MEN OF MYSTERY
NIKOLA TESLA And OTIS T. CARR

By
Timothy Green Beckley
&
Tim R. Swartz

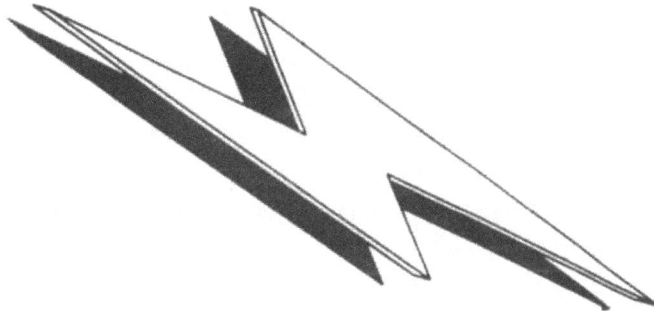

GLOBAL COMMUNICATIONS

Men of Mystery
Nikola Tesla and Otis T. Carr
By Timothy Green Beckley & Tim R. Swartz

This edition layout and design copyright © 2012
DBA Global Communications – All Rights Reserved

ISBN-10: 1-60611-123-X
ISBN-13: 978-1-60611-123-9

Non-Fiction

Printed in the United States of America

Timothy Green Beckley: Editorial Director
Carol Ann Rodriguez: Publishers Assistant
Editor & Graphics: Tim R. Swartz
Sean Casteel: Associate Editor
William Kern: Associate Editor

For Free Subscription to the Conspiracy Journal Write:
Tim Beckley/Global Communications
Box 753
New Brunswick, NJ 08903

Sign Up On Line: MRUFO8@hotmail.com

www.ConspiracyJournal.Com

Contents

TESLA - MORE MYSTERIOUS THAN EVER BEFORE!
By Timothy Green Beckley

THE original edition of this little work on the great genius Nikola Tesla was years ahead of its time. When first published several decades ago, there was little interested readers could reference on this most remarkable man. I do believe our niche publishing enterprise was the first to broach the topic of Tesla's marvelous genius. There was maybe one biography and a couple of old monographs that were published on Tesla's patents in a very unpolished form.

Today, there are many works on Tesla available. Some good and some missing the mark altogether. You can divide the hundreds of reference works into two major categories -- the first being books that are based on historical, well established, facts about Nikola's life and scientific discovers. The other books would contain what we can call "fringe material" about Tesla's supposed birth on another planet, his communications with "Martians" and spirit beings.

The author of Man of Mystery, Michael X, looks at Tesla's other-worldly involvement in a sober manner, but is willing to test and accept new ideas about an individual that most of us know so little about.

There are those who believe that much of Tesla's discoveries have yet to be released. That at the time of his death his New Yorker hotel room was broken into and many folders containing his most confidential works were whisked away to an unknown destination, perhaps Wright Patterson Air Force Base in Ohio. Those wishing to delve into these possibilities should by all means grab up a copy of Tim R. Swartz's Lost Journal's of Nikola Tesla for all the material on Tesla that might have been hushed up by the CIA and other agencies, supposedly attempting to keep his "secrets" out of the hands of enemy operatives.

In any regards, this work should be as well received today as when it first saw the light of day. Michael X walks into the shadows and emerges into the light with some remarkable proclamations on the man we all want to know so much about.
Join us in our search for the truth about Nikola Tesla and Otis T. Carr, Men of Mystery.

Tim Beckley, Publisher
MrUFO8@hotmail.com

IF we read the usual school textbooks, we are told we know who Nikola Tesla really was. But we are told only that he discovered the principle of alternating current (the ordinary "A.C." house current you utilize in your home). Some books may briefly sketch out some of Tesla's work in the field of static electricity, and other "conventional" fields.

What we are NOT told is that Tesla also carried out experiments and devised plans for inventions, not only "ahead of their time" in that day—but which even today would be termed "science fiction" devices by the uninitiated.

During his latter work on this plane, Tesla was secretive about most of his inventions, even to his close friends and students. It is alleged that immediately after his death, his files were seized by a certain Agency, which to this day, keeps these secrets locked away from their use by mankind, because of fears of Vested Interests that the development of these inventions might cause them economic ruin.

It is believed by many students of Tesla that this same Agency, never mentioned publicly in any publication or broadcast, is the very same one which has suppressed vital information about the presence of UFO and space people among us. Also, it is They, these students aver, who have been responsible for silencing many UFO investigators.

Perhaps we will never know who Nikola Tesla really was. Some have speculated that he was brought here as an infant from another planet, others contend that he was a mystic who based his inventions upon hunches and phantom images which constantly floated through his mind.

But whoever Nikola Tesla was he was definitely a man without a century. His discoveries, and impact on society are just today being felt.

During his lifetime he was scorned and abused by 95% of the scientific community, a community to which he felt he could help and contribute.

Whether Tesla was a spaceman or not we may probably never be able to prove. But we do know that he took an exceptional interest in the possibility of life on other planets and their future implications on our society. He even claimed to have received messages from "out there", and some of his pupils claim that he was in constant touch with interplanetary beings who were responsible for imparting some of his marvelous inventions to him by means of telepathic and verbal messages.

During the latter days of his life he was even said to have been interested in astral travel and in the possibility of life after death. And although much of this cannot be checked out we do have brief mentions of his "supernormal" interests in much of what he wrote.

The *AMERICAN MAGAZINE* sent a reporter to see Tesla in 1921 and he told the reporter, a Mr.

M.K. Wisehart, how "During my boyhood I suffered from a particular affliction due to the appearance of images, which were often accompanied by strong flashes of light. When a word was spoken, the image of the object designated would present itself so vividly to my vision that I could not tell whether what I saw was real or not. . .Even though I reached out and passed my hand through the image, it would remain fixed in space."

Others throughout the years have written of their experiences with Tesla but none have really been very specific when it came to the part about his interest in otherworldly communications.

However one Arthur H. Matthews, now living in Canada, worked under Tesla during the time in which communications apparently were coming through on a regular basis. In fact Matthews helped construct THE TESLA SCOPE FOR SPACE COMMUNICATION, a diagram of which appears in print in this volume for the first time.

The information you are about to read has been communicated to me through friends on both your physical, and OTHER planes, to which I am attuned.

AN INVENTION THAT COULD SAVE OUR PLANET

THE following is a communication received from a student who has now departed the Earth Plane and who is one of the Mentors assisting advanced New Age thinkers on that Plane.

This student is well known to many of our readers but is not named here for reasons we cannot reveal at this time:

In the fateful year of 1856 a space ship set out from Venus on a mission to the planet Earth. As the ship neared the Earth, an event took place which was to change the entire course of scientific development on this planet. A baby boy was born on board the ship, and the space people gave him the name of Nikola. At midnight, between July 9th and 10th, the space ship landed in a remote section of an Austro-Hungarian province which is today known as Yugoslavia. The child Nikola was taken to the home of a young married couple, a man and woman of goodwill, as the space people described them. The tiny Venusian prodigy was entrusted to their care.to the Rev. Milutin Tesla and his wife, Djouka. He grew up as their son, Nikola Tesla, a babe from Venus. His foster parents guarded well the secret of his birth, even when he later received worldwide recognition as Nikola Tesla, the superman. This secret has now been disclosed by the space people themselves, for they now desire that we understand more about the persons they have infiltrated into our population to aid us in our hour of need.

Tesla died in New York City during the night of January 7, 1943, and it was thought by many that his earthly work was finished. The forces of darkness rejoiced at news of his death which they considered was most opportune. The world was at war, and under pressure of this need, the patents of Tesla were considered as royal plunder. The very gifts of genius which had been intended to preserve us from wars were used to satisfy the greed, the passions, and the hatreds of the evil forces.

But darkness never wins out over Light, and now, according to the space people, the real work of Tesla is about to begin, for it is part of the Divine Plan for humanity on this earth that we enjoy in full abundance the new way of life which Tesla's inventions will bring us. Tesla was just one man, just one Venusian, who lived on this planet for 87 years. He was a scientist in the field of electrical development. Yet his inventions alone, if developed, will automatically solve every immediate need of humanity on the physical plane, leaving mankind free and at peace to develop his full soul expression.

Tesla's inventions, if developed, will make nuclear experiments obsolete; they will render warfare impossible, making each country safe within its borders, free to develop its particular culture in peace and harmony; they will open up interplanetary communication to everyone immediately; they will permit the space people to send us teachers who can train the entire population of this planet in every phase of art, philosophy, science, and Universal Law, known in this solar system. All of this and much, much more can be accomplished by the simple expedient of utilizing the inventions of Nikola Tesla.

And what can you do to further this project, this phase of the Divine Plan? You can demand, demand, demand that the inventions of Tesla be utilized. Ask and you shall receive. This is a Divine promise. Therefore, ask! Spread this word to the ends of the earth, this immediate answer to our immediate problem. If you can understand the technical aspects of these Tesla inventions, by all means study the writings on the subject, and inform yourself. But if your best efforts do not lie along scientific lines, then just seek to understand the desperate need of humanity for help in this hour, and know in your heart that help is at hand.

Spread these tidings of joy!

Those of you who are yearning to see space ships in the sky, to talk to the people in those ships, to receive messages, to receive comfort, assurance, and some guarantee of security, please stop and consider. There are thousands of space people here with us now, but if you complain that you do not know any of them, that you cannot recognize them, then find comfort in the fact that Nikola Tesla of Venus was with us on this planet, in a physical body, for 87 years; he is still with us today in his subtle body. He is a practical man who has devoted his life to the greatest salvage operation that we have known on this planet since the time of Jesus. Indeed, it was Jesus Himself who said that we, in our time, would do greater things than He could do for us 2000 years ago because of our limited knowledge then.

Let us now consider just what is being done about the Tesla inventions, the attitude of the space people toward the Tesla project, and the scope of the inventions themselves.

So vast is the scientific field explored by Tesla that it is difficult to classify the work of this superman. He was not an inventor in the usual sense; he was a discoverer; the universe was his laboratory. To say that he harnessed electricity for use on a world scale is totally inadequate.

This was the man who envisioned a world-wide wireless power system, not for any one nation or group, but for all of God's children. He invented alternating current to replace the limited use of direct current, and then he harnessed Niagara Falls to supply electricity. At the age of 80 years, his wireless-power system was still to be developed, as today, but he did not resent the delay. "Perhaps I was a little premature," he said, "but meanwhile my polyphase alternating current system continues to meet our needs to lighten the burdens of mankind and increase comfort and happiness. Just as soon as the need arises I have the wireless system ready to be used with complete success."

Like the spaceman that he was, Tesla knew that he could only encourage us; he could not force his light upon us; he could only respect our free will.

Nevertheless he knew that his alternating current (A.C.) system had made the power age possible, but he also knew that it had made World Wars I and II possible. Being a man of goodwill he sought to properly curb the mighty force he had unleashed in the world, so he invented, in 1935, an anti-war machine, as he called it. This anti-war machine could have been put into effect all over the world, and it would have made each country safe within its borders. It would have ended all aggression between nations. It would not have ended family and community squabbles inside national borders. . .or would it? Perhaps. Who knows what course human evolution might have taken if, say, by 1935, all fear of warfare had been removed from the world?

Remember that the space people have had vast experience in guiding other planets in other solar systems through emergencies exactly like the difficulty which faces us now. They estimate that even with their help and our unlimited cooperation, it may require about fifty years to complete the task of establishing God's kingdom on earth. They base this timing on actual results recently achieved in another solar system where the planetary problems were very similar to ours.

However, they feel that we can probably progress more rapidly because we are far more developed along artistic lines, and therefore have greater imaginative and intuitive powers than our friends in the neighboring solar system.

The Tesla anti-war machine was not utilized in 1935, nor by 1955, nor at the present date; so the fear of warfare has not been removed from the world. Would you like to have the fear of warfare removed from the world now? Then go right ahead and demand your God-given heritage of human brotherhood. You can demand that human security be preserved, human dignity and human rights assured, by making all national borders secure by the installation of the Tesla anti-war machine. But your demands will have to be loud, very loud indeed, for the forces of darkness do not like to hear the sound of the voices of men and women of goodwill. Remember, too, that certain governments of the world were offered this invention of Tesla himself, away back in 1935, and his offers were spurned. Great fortunes were to be made. Nothing could interfere with that. . .nothing that is, except the voice of the people themselves.

But uninformed people are silent people, and so the bloody course of history, which might have been changed, was not changed.

There is another reason why the people were not told about the anti-war machine. Tesla had invented polyphase alternating current in his youth, as a sort of stop-gap, so that people everywhere could have the immediate use of electricity, since direct current could be used only within an area of one square mile around each power station. Tesla did not intend that we should still be using an old-fashioned, complicated system of wiring and electrical distribution today. But he first had to invent a wireless method. He did this and the radio was an offshoot, a by-product of Tesla's experiments.

When he did come forward with his world wireless power system, the forces of darkness, securely entrenched behind the world's financial interests, would have none of it. One of the greatest financiers in the United States listened to Tesla himself describe the glories of his invention, and then the financier dismissed the whole subject as impractical because, as the money baron pointed out, there would be no way of making money off the people, if the people could have all the electricity they wanted by merely sticking up a little antenna on their homes, factories, or office buildings. This astute financier pointed out that under the present system the manufacturers of wires, poles, and electrical installation equipment of all kinds, could make fortunes, and in addition the electricity could be metered and everybody could be charged for every kilowatt they used.

Tesla pointed out that electricity was free in the atmosphere, a gift of God to his people, but such idealism naturally could not penetrate the thinking of the financier.

If today we demand Tesla's invention of wireless electrical distribution, we can still have all the electricity we want by merely sticking up a little antenna on our homes and other buildings. But his is the catch. . .Tesla's anti-war machine is based on the same idea.it requires no poles, no wires, no reflectors, no platforms, no micro-wave towers, no walls or fences.

Now, if we are to have this New Age cake, we will naturally want the frosting too. This means that we can have protection along all national boundary lines without a single wall, wire, tower or any similar device. It also means that we have no further need for any kind of poles, towers, cables, reflectors or wires for electricity, telephones, telegraph, radios or television. Then, since we would have national boundary protection, and positive protection for all coasts, we could do away with the army, the navy, and the marines.

If you have doubted that Tesla was a Venusian, this is a fairly safe spot to cast aside your doubts.

And if you will reflect upon this report you will realize that the space people mean business. They are collaborators with the Creator of the Universe, and when they tell us to give up warfare they mean for us to give up warfare! Many persons have been murmuring, "But how could we give up warfare, with those awful Communists ready to attack us?"

The space people have a huge space station which orbits the earth, and which cannot be tracked by radar (another Tesla invention which will be mentioned later.) The reason is because the space station is equipped with extremely delicate instruments which might be damaged by radar.

These instruments not only record all words spoken upon the earth, but they also record all thought patterns. The murmurings mentioned above naturally came to the attention of the space people, and they want to know why we are concerned about other nations attacking us when we are free to use the Tesla invention any time we wish. Not only along our own borders, but along all borders, so as to quiet all fears which make for aggression. This invention is not something to be kept secret. On the contrary, we must insist that all nations use it for mutual protection.

Although it is called an anti-war machine, it is not, properly speaking, a machine. It is more like a magnetic or polarized curtain of air. For your information, a similar protective vibratory curtain has been in operation for thousand of years in certain places on this planet, areas regarded as sacred or holy places. This very weekend, at the time of the Taurus Full Moon, the annual Wesak Festival is being celebrated in the Wesak Valley in Tibet. During this ancient ceremony, performed each year in the Wesak Valley, Gautama, the Buddha comes back to the earth for one day from his present home on the star Sirius. He returns annually to greet his friend and collaborator, the Lord Maitreya, the Christ, together with the assembled Masters of Wisdom who constitute the Spiritual Hierarchy on this planet.

The Wesak Valley in Tibet has been guarded through the centuries by an invisible magnetic curtain. No human being ever finds his way into this sacred valley unless he is a person of goodwill, a soul dedicated to the welfare of humanity. According to the Divine Plan for this solar system, the time has now come when this entire globe is to become a Sacred Planet; that is why the space people are here to help us, to bring about a state of heaven on earth, for on a sacred planet there can be no warfare; there cannot even be a consciousness of ill-will in the minds and hearts of the inhabitants.

We have mentioned radar, and it is important that we consider this for a moment. Let us clearly understand that scientists and technicians all over the world have never under-estimated the Tesla inventions. Many scientists regarded them with humble admiration; but alas, very often they have been evaluated in an atmosphere strongly tinged with a lurid green shade of envy. Efforts have been made almost constantly, even during Tesla's lifetime in a physical body, to "grab-off" his ideas and try to copy them at a handsome profit, of course. Tesla invented genuine radar as a part, a very small functional part, of another invention, the anti-war machine. He never intended that radar should function separately, isolated from the anti-war machine.

After the anti-war machine was rejected, some of the scientific minds of our country tried to develop, from hearsay, a small portion of the original invention. They did not have the necessary facts and the result is radar as we know it today.

Scientists admit that it does not work very well. It works just as well as an automobile tire without a wheel; it works as well as an electric light without a light bulb. What more can anybody expect from a fragment of a piece of a machine that was never built?

In 1938 Tesla announced that he had developed a method for interplanetary communication. When Tesla died in 1943 this country was at war, and his papers were removed from the safe in his room and sealed by government authorities.

Nothing more was heard of his work in this country except for the valuable information contained in a biography which was published in 1944, a book entitled **Prodigal Genius** by John J. O'Neill, then science editor of the New York Herald Tribune. O'Neill has since died. As a reporter, O'Neill had long been an acquaintance of

Tesla's, but Tesla had never taken O'Neill into his confidence, because O'Neill did not have a sound background in occult studies. He very much desired to probe the ancient mysteries, to study the philosophy of the East and the Ageless Wisdom, and he recognized Tesla as a man whose mind was more at home on the esoteric plane than on the physical plane. Tesla himself never worked freely in physical matter. His machines were all designed in the ether, for he was completely clairvoyant. He not only designed and molded his machines in etheric substance; but he tested the etheric models and made any adjustments required.

He never made any notes, drawings or specifications, for he had the power of instant recall. Only in later years, when he was preparing to shed his physical form, did he write out notes and specifications for the aid of his engineers who would continue his work on the physical plane.

When Tesla died in 1943 O'Neill assumed that the work of the superman was over; he stated that Tesla left no "disciples" to carry on. But Tesla left many disciples; many close associates to whom he entrusted all his important notes, drawings, and secrets. The papers left in his safe were purposely placed there to satisfy idle curiosity. Nothing of importance was allowed to fall into greedy hands.

He left complete instructions for the building of the machine for interplanetary communication.

The machine was built after his death and placed in operation in 1950. It will not pick up any broadcasts from radio stations on earth, but is designed to receive broadcasts from space ships, and can be equipped to receive from other planets if that should become necessary. When Tesla left instructions for the building of the machine, he said that some day in the near future space ships would be approaching the earth, and it would be nice to have the machine so that we could talk to the space people.

After the machine was placed in operation, broadcasts were received frequently from space ships, and then shortly thereafter the space ships landed near the home of the owner of the machine.

The space visitors were made welcome, and now they frequently visit and chat with the Tesla engineers. The first space ship which landed was 700 feet in diameter, 300 feet high, with a center tube fifty feet in diameter. It held 24 smaller ships, 75 to 100 feet in diameter, and it came from Venus.

It seems apparent that persons who are contacted by space people are usually assigned to some certain phase of the work, something for which they are equipped. Also their work on behalf of the space people seems to follow a certain pattern determined by the space people themselves. For some reason the Tesla phase of the work is just now beginning. Those involved in this particular project are now being placed in communication with each other, and the space people want the inventions developed, but they want them developed in response to a voiced demand from the earth people. Remember that we have to use our free will to get things accomplished. God will work with us, but He will certainly not work for us.

The space people regret that we sit back and wait for our governments or experts or authorities to thrust some development upon us, just anything at all, from chemical fertilizer to a full-scale war.

The space people insist that we search our hearts, ask Divine guidance, determine our needs, demand, and then gratefully receive. Let us demand whatever we need to live as free and joyous children of God! Let us demand whatever we need to carry out the Divine Plan of establishing God's Kingdom on the Planet Earth!

Original Caption: "Nikola Tesla holding in his hands balls of flame." Tesla's accident in 1895 may have led to his later Dynamic Theory of Gravity in which gravity is described as a "field effect." The presence of highly charged, rotating magnetic fields could therefore influence time/space within a localized area.

THE TESLA SCOPE
FOR SPACE
COMMUNICATIONS

MANY years ago, long before the days when to many of us the idea of communication with other planets was strictly a Buck Rogers fantasy, Nikola Tesla was already conducting serious research experiments and inventing devices for communication with intelligent life on other planets. Furthermore, he was the first man in Earth's history to record receiving what he firmly believed to be intelligently controlled signals from outer space.

The illustration on page 22 has been copied from a rough sketch (not to scale) drawn by Arthur H. Matthews of the basic concept of the design for a Space Communication Set which would increase the speed of electrical waves to 27 times that of light, as first conceived by Nikola Tesla in 1898, with the objective of communicating with the

Planet Venus. Due to pressures of other work, however, the first working model was not built by Tesla until 1918. In 1938, Arthur H. Matthews, under Tesla's guidance, built an improved version of this device at Sanford, in the Province of Quebec, Canada. In 1947, three years after Tesla's death, he re-built the Set, incorporating further improvements and finally, in 1967, he re-constructed the Tesla Scope, adapting the new micro-miniature electronics and reducing its size to 6 ft. long and 4 in diameter. While the more recent models have incorporated the refinements of modem technology, this Space Communication Set retains the same basic concept as originally devised by Nikola Tesla and by this means, Mr. Matthews has, over the years, received messages from space people who claim that they are from Venus.

In the following pages we present a communication from Mr. Matthews regarding these messages:

I am told that the following message purporting to come from Venus, has been transmitted through various channels to the people of Earth for many hundreds of years. It is, in the main, the same message which I have received via the Tesla Scope in the years 1941, 1945, 1947, 1949, 1951, 1957, 1959 and 1961. This same message has been repeated because the same conditions exist on Earth. When I first received it in 1941, I was informed that it came from space people who claimed to be from Venus and who were aboard a spacecraft they called the X-12, a mother-ship 700 ft. in diameter and 300 ft. in height. They told me that if I visualized two saucers put together, with a tube in the centre and a separate ring around the outside, I would have some idea of the shape of this spacecraft which, they stated, carried 24 smaller spaceships inside exactly like the mother-ship except they were from 50 to 100 feet in diameter. They claimed that their spacecraft were operated solely by means of thought waves and that they had no other power, no motors or other forms of propulsion such as Earth people use.

Apart from the omission of certain personal messages connected mainly with my continued work for Tesla on Earth, the following is the message I first received in 1941 and which, in essence, has been repeated over the years.

"When you first receive this message, you will, like most Earth people, doubt. This is one of the strange things we find about the people of Earth, their continued doubting. They say they believe in God, but they doubt. They say God can cure their sicknesses and their troubles, but they doubt. Therefore, we expect you to doubt also. You will wonder if we really come from Venus, do we come from outer space? And you will wonder how we are able to talk to you in your own language. We use English at this time because you, our friend Matthews, only understand this language, but we have made a study of every language used by mankind. Actually, we would prefer to transmit our thoughts by the use of mental waves which would activate the Tesla machine.

"As we look down on Earth, we note the greatest confusion and misunderstanding. Instead of acknowledging the One God and looking towards Him for enlightenment, we find you all over the Earth running hopelessly and helplessly in pursuit of many things you think will increase your personal happiness, and yet you wonder why you continue to suffer. We hear all of you, year after year, asking the same questions...Why must we suffer? Why do we still have wars, sickness, poverty, famine and death? Why does pure joy always run away faster than we can, so that we can never catch up with it?

"The answers to these questions are to be found in the fact that instead of turning upwards to God, your thoughts are earthbound and you judge only by what you see in others around you, the vast majority of whom are sick, unhappy and full of bad habits, doubting the existence of the Supreme Being and futilely, you follow the group. Your Earth is full of hate and misery and this condition has come to be accepted as the rule for mankind on Earth. This is not how God intended life to be on your beautiful planet, but very few of you obey the Laws of God. Many of you attend some form of religious service on your Sundays, but how many Earth people carry out God's Laws in their everyday lives? We are amazed and saddened to find how much of your time is devoted to inventing and using destructive machines with which you murder each other. We see you spending vast sums of money pretending to bring peace on Earth, when you should know that the only way of obtaining peace is free, through Christ Love, there is no other way, so why waste your money and energy? We ask this question realizing that most Earth people have known for almost 2,000 years that the only way to secure peace on Earth and goodwill towards your fellow men is by following the teachings of Jesus Christ whom a God of Love sent to your planet to bring spiritual enlightenment to mankind.

"Therefore, we can only sadly conclude that the Earth people must be suffering from some form of mental sickness which can only be cured in one way, the way of the Christ Philosophy of Love. You have heard all this before and much of what we say will fall on deaf ears, but our thoughts are directed to those few of the Earth people who have sufficient mental and spiritual power to think clearly and to know right from wrong. These few have been implanted among you to help others to evolve spiritually and to grow in a manner to be of service to the Great, All-Knowing, All-Loving God and all His creatures. Your present behavior is the reason for the continued visits to Earth by those of the space people who endeavour to act as spiritual guardians to your planet, but we must warn you that if you continue to conduct your lives by wrong thinking, you will surely annihilate yourselves—and we shall not have many people to pick up when your Earth is about to be destroyed.

"To help the people of Earth, we brought down one of our own to live among you. During a trip from our planet to Earth, a Venusian child was born. We landed our spacecraft at midnight on July 9, 1856 and decided to leave this boy-child in the care of a good man and his wife. This infant was Nikola Tesla and we left him on Earth in the hope that his higher mental powers and inventive genius would enable him to build advanced machines for the benefit of humanity and that your world, torn by hate and wars, would thereby come out of the darkness into the light. During the years between 1856 and 1943, we landed many times on Earth, but we found no improvement there. At the death of Tesla in 1943, we landed again and attended his funeral. We were saddened to find that the Earth people had used the gifts of Tesla and other great inventors only to satisfy their greed and lust for power, that the same evil conditions existed on Earth and that its people continued to expend their energy on wars and killing their own kind, which is contrary to God's Law which clearly states: Thou shalt not kill.

"These things are beyond our understanding for Venus, in all its history, has never had war. We have but one purpose in life—to serve God and this we do with all our energy of body and mind and because we do this, our mental power grows stronger with age. We remain in perfect health until the day we die. We enjoy perfect harmony, health and happiness with our loved ones all the days of our lives. We have no place in our hearts for selfish desires because we know and believe that God's Law is good and therefore we have no need for man-made laws.

"Lack of faith in God has left your Earth in the Dark Ages and you will never progress or know peace of mind, true happiness and complete harmony until you learn to renew your faith and to become higher in your thinking and living than the crawling things which you now appear to emulate—instead of becoming spiritually-minded beings in the likeness of God. To avert hatred and wars, you must learn to remove every trace of national pride and racial discrimination, for there is, in fact, only one race in the entire Universe—that of mankind whom God created."

In support of Mr. Matthews' words, we would like to present the following condensed extract from "*Understanding*" (a magazine we can highly recommend), which describes some of Tesla's early experiences with the space communication.

"In the year 1899, Nikola Tesla, with the aid of his financial backer, millionaire J.P. Morgan, set up at Colorado Springs, an experimental laboratory containing high voltage radio transmission equipment, a 200-ft. tower for transmission and reception of radio waves and the best receiving equipment available at that time. One night, when he was alone in the laboratory, he observed what he cautiously referred to as 'electrical actions which definitely appeared to be signals.' The changes were taking place periodically and with such a clear suggestion of number and order that they could not be traced to any cause then known to him.

In a written report, Tesla stated, "I was familiar, of course, with such electrical disturbances as are produced by the sun, the Aurora Borealis and earth currents, and I am as sure as I can be of any fact, that these "variations" were due to none of these causes. It was some time afterward, however, that the thought flashed upon me that the disturbances might be due to intelligent control. The feeling is growing constantly upon me that I had been the first to hear the greeting of one planet to another!"

THE TESLA SCOPE FOR SPACE COMMUNICATION

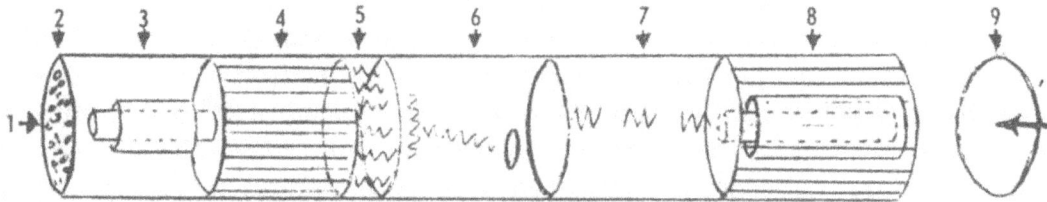

"Q" Glass Vacuum Tube enclosed in wooden box
9 ft. long, 5" in diameter

Legend:
(1) Audio Output. (2) Pick up. (3) Converter. (4) Automatic Control Chamber.
(5) Gas Chamber. (6) Converter. (7) Received Energy Control. (8) Dark Room (this
section enclosed in pure silver shield). (9) Head.

The Teslascope was a radio transmitter designed by Nikola Tesla with the intention of communicating with other planets. It received publicity after Tesla's statement on the device was published by Time Magazine in their July 20, 1931 issue celebrating Tesla's 75th birthday.

[I have conceived] a means that will make it possible for man to transmit energy in large amounts, thousands of horsepower, from one planet to another, absolutely regardless of distance. I think that nothing can be more important than interplanetary communication. It will certainly come some day. and the certitude that there are other human beings in the universe, working, suffering, struggling, like ourselves, will produce a magic effect on mankind and will form the foundation of a universal brotherhood that will last as long as humanity itself.

—Nikola Tesla

THE TESLA
SPACE DRIVE

WE recently received a set of plans from a former pupil of Nikola Tesla who believes that a space ship, working on the principles of the "flying saucers," can actually be constructed.

He bases his plans, he told us, upon existing files he secretly obtained shortly before Tesla's death, and before these could be seized by the authorities.

He and Tesla had been very close friends and had worked together on a number of projects. This pupil, however, told us that we must not reveal his name, since his work with the invention is yet in the experimental stages. He also warned us that the principles used in this invention could actually be harmful and very dangerous, considering the "field effect" which he describes as an "anti-electromagnetic field drive."

Although the basic scientific principles are technical, we feel these should be presented to the reader as a matter of record. We have shown this document to a few persons whose scientific knowledge is great, and have been told that the principles advanced in the Tesla Space Drive are sound. They, too, however, warned us of the dangers involved.

The accompanying diagram shows the general arrangement of components in a test device designed to demonstrate the procedure for developing a "one-body system".

Before outlining this procedure, I shall explain what I mean by the terms rotation and gyration since both terms appear in the outline to follow and both have very specific meaning for me. In order to understand my use of these terms one must understand the meanings I attach to them. I do not see gyration as a form of angular motion or rotation but as a form of translatory or linear motion. While gyration simulates rotation it is not true rotation. True rotation is two-dimensional and in order to rotate an object must display radial depth. In a rotating object all component particles travel in circular objects of varying radius about centerpoints lying in a single straight line called the axis of rotation. The range of variation in length of the orbit radii is the radial depth of the object. In the gyrating object (as I think of gyration and use the term) all the component particles again travel in circular orbits. In this case, however, all orbits have the same radius and their centerpoints do not all lie on a single straight line. There is no common axis, no concentricity, and therefore no radial depth.

The first step in developing this system is to cause a counter-clockwise (sense chosen arbitrarily) acceleration of the center of mass of the four eccentrics in a circular orbit about the X axis. This must be done without generating a clockwise reaction about the X axis.

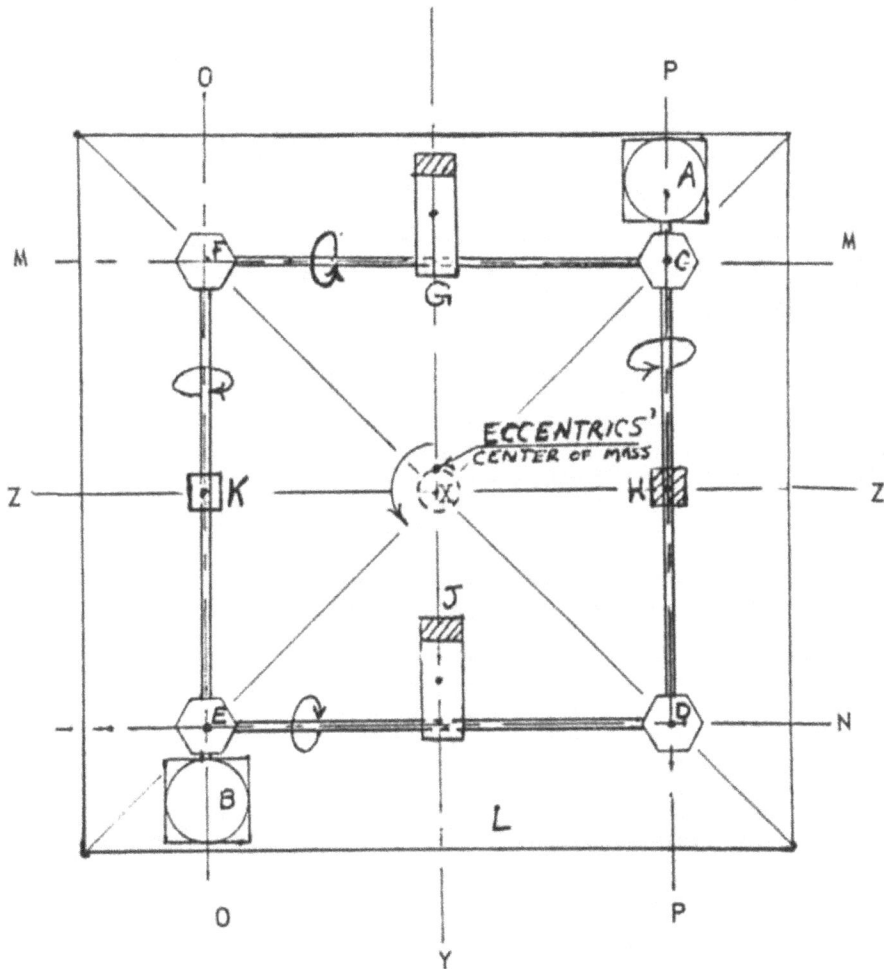

Key:

A and B are motors (should be identical)

C, D, E and F are right-angle drives 1:1 ratio

G, H, J, and K are eccentrics

L is the base plate to which the motors, gear boxes, and pillow blocks (not shown) are fastened

M, N, O, and P are the axes of rotation of eccentrics G, H, J, and K

Y and Z are the planes of rotation of the eccentrics

X is the line of intersection of planes Y and Z

These conditions can be met by introducing angular acceleration of the eccentrics about their respective axes of rotation, M, N, O, and P. Of course this will produce a gyratory reaction upon the rest of the device but this gyration is also counter-clockwise. Now there is a common point about which the center of mass of the eccentrics and the center of mass of the device as a whole gyrate but these centers are points without radial depth even though they vary in radius of orbit. The center of gyration always lies directly between them. They represent two opposed radii; and because each radius is represented by a point they have no depth.

We have two points traveling in circular orbits about a third point. If we project a straight line through this third point parallel to the X axis we have what I shall call the system axis. The X axis of course is simply the line of intersection of planes Y and Z (refer to Key). The system axis relates the two components of what I shall call the typically opposed interaction. This is the kind of interaction manifested in this type of "one-body system."

With all components of the system gyrating in a counter-clockwise direction about the system axis we have a SIMULATION of counter-clockwise rotation about this axis with no corresponding clockwise rotation. In the process of creating this situation, however, we have introduced genuine counter-clockwise angular acceleration about the system axis. Referring to the diagram, note the sense of the rotation of the eccentrics about their respective axis and their positions relative to L.

The angular accelerations exerted upon H and K produce hub reactions which are linear accelerations toward the right. These accelerations are transmitted by L to the hubs of G and J. The inertial resistance of G and J to these accelerations will of course act in the opposite direction or toward the left and can be represented as forces acting at the centers of mass of these two eccentrics. This means that there is a counter-clockwise force couple acting on both G and J, and these force couples are transmitted to the system as a whole. Therefore, the entire system is subject to a counter-clockwise torque about the system axis. There is no corresponding clockwise torque.

The reaction to this angular acceleration is a linear acceleration along the system axis and directed outward from the page. This typically opposed interaction is similar to the one which causes the electron to move about the nucleus of the atom. The electron, however, functions in accordance with the left-hand rule and this system functions in accordance with the right-hand rule.

Although the atomic nucleus is usually passive or inert in the spatial sense, it possesses a latent capacity for regulating its spatial displacement. It takes very special conditions to incite the nucleus to an exercise of this power, but this device sets up those conditions. The nucleus cannot regulate its rate of spatial displacement but it can under certain conditions initiate a change in the directional quality of this displacement. The one-way angular acceleration created by this system causes the nuclei of the system to react.

The axial acceleration of the system is really a side effect caused by the nuclei swerving from their paths in an effort to abolish the field effect caused by the one-way torque. Since they cannot slow themselves down this swerving aside is the only way they can neutralize the effects of the field.

The axial thrust of this device is superimposed upon a wobble-plate effect which is a side-effect of the angular acceleration of the eccentrics about their respective axis. In the positions shown in the diagram the hub reaction initiated by G will thrust its side of L into the page while the hub reaction of J will thrust its side of L out of the page. This produces a torque upon L and the axis of this angular acceleration rotates counter-clockwise about the system axis. As a result this field drive will exhibit a peculiar tendency to wobble noticeably at low thrust levels. This effect fades out, however, as the thrust is increased.

This field drive can be used to propel space ships. Whether such space ships would be fit for human habitation, however, or whether they would be deadly I can not say.

THE MAN WHO COULD PHOTOGRAPH THOUGHTS

EVEN in his own day, Nikola Tesla was considered a genius.his accomplishments went way beyond any known form of science. This clipping, from a 1933 edition of the *Kansas City Post*, shows his futuristic mental process.

PROVING HIS THEORY that a man's efficiency and accomplishments should increase and not diminish with mellow age, Nikola Tesla, inventor, physicist and one of the world's leading electrical technicians, enters his seventy-eighth year busily engaged on three- or four great scientific projects.

Several of these inventions or discoveries will be looked upon as "miracles" by many people, for Mr. Tesla has long been a scientist years ahead of his time, one whose advanced theories have alternately stamped him a "madman" and a wizard.

Just as people ridiculed Copernicus' theory of the planetary system, the unenlightened jeered Tesla's pronouncement, years ago, regarding cosmic rays. The pathfinder and the pioneer, and Mr. Tesla is both, are always condemned by the masses.

Nikola Tesla, tall, lean, with the face of an ascetic and deep-set eyes, whose expression denotes concentration on a canvas of work too big for most people's comprehension, partially described a new and inexhaustible source of power he has discovered after years of research, revolutionizing modern physical science. At the same time he touched on his own reservoir of energy which makes such monumental discoveries possible at his advanced age.

How does he tap both these deep wells? What is the secret of fine health, keen mind, unusual vitality and mental force at 77, the time of life when most men are sitting in the sun with shawls over their knees or, alas, lying beneath the sod?

Mr. Tesla is the father of the alternating system of power transmission and radio, the induction motor and Tesla coil.

Asked about his startling new scientific discoveries, one of which concerns the "photographing of thought," which will, he maintains, bring about a tremendous social revolution, he said, "My first and most important discovery concerns the harnessing of a new source of power, hitherto unavailable, to be developed through fundamentally novel machines of my invention. I am not yet prepared to dwell on the details of the project, for they must be checked before my findings can be formally announced. I have worked on the development of the underlying principles for many years. From the practical point of view of the engineer engaged in power development, the first investment will be relatively very great, but once a machine is installed it may be depended on to function indefinitely, and the cost of operation will be next to nothing.

"My power generator will be of the simplest kind .just a big mass of steel, copper and aluminum, comprising a stationary and rotating part, peculiarly assembled. I am planning to develop electricity and transmit it to a distance by my alternating system now universally established. The direct current system could also be employed if the heretofore insuperable difficulties of insulating the transmission lines can be overcome.

"Such a source of power obtainable everywhere will solve many problems with which the human race is confronted. My alternating system has been the means of harnessing 30,000,000 horsepower of waterpower, and there are projects now going on all over the world which will eventually double that amount. But, unfortunately, there is not enough waterpower to satisfy present needs, and everywhere inventors and engineers are endeavoring to unlock some additional store of energy."

Will the smashing of the atom lead to this new power energy? Let Mr. Tesla answer, "The public is naturally led to expect a great revolution through the harnessing of atomic power, but this is an illusion. Atomic energy is not available for work. I operated many years ago apparatus of a capacity of 2,000 horsepower and tension of 18,000,000 volts with which trillions of atoms were smashed in a fraction of a second. I generated all sorts of intense and destructive rays, but found no trace of any energy which should have been liberated through the shattering of atomic structures, according to theory. For the last thirty years I have warned my fellow scientists that there is nothing to be expected in this field except some specific effects due to changes in the atomic structure which may have more or less value."

Beyond adding that the new form of energy which he has been investigating many years would be available at any place in the world in unlimited quantities, and that the machinery for harnessing it would last more than 5,000 years, Mr. Tesla would say little more on the subject. Just when the power will become available for practical purposes he could not predict with any degree of precision. In a few years, perhaps, he ventured to say.

Mr. Tesla then talked of several other projects on which he has been working by way of relief from too much concentration on the main place of work. He described one of his other interests, one highly dramatic, which stirs the imagination and which, doubtless, will sound too revolutionary to most people.

But it must not be forgotten, as Mr. Tesla points out, that the ideas of television and radio and airplane were scoffed at in their infancy. "I expect to photograph thoughts," announced Mr. Tesla calmly, in the same tone of voice that a person occupied with some trivial things in the scheme of life might announce that it was going to rain.

Continued Mr. Tesla: "In 1893, while engaged in certain investigations, I became convinced that a definite image formed in thought must, by reflex action, produce a corresponding image on the retina, which might possibly be read by suitable apparatus. This brought me to my system of television, which I announced at that time.

"My idea was to employ an artificial retina receiving the image of the object seen, an 'optic nerve' and another such retina at the place of reproduction. These two retinas were to be constructed somewhat after the fashion of a checkerboard, with many separate little sections, and the so-called optic nerve was nothing more than a part of the earth.

"An invention of mine enables me to transmit simultaneously, and without any interference whatsoever, hundreds of thousands of distinct impulses through the ground just as though I had so many separate wires. I did not contemplate using any moving part, a scanning apparatus or a cathodic ray, which is a sort of moving device, the use of which I suggested in one of my lectures of that period.

"Now if it be true that a thought reflects an image on the retina, it is a mere question of illuminating the same properly and taking photographs, and then using the ordinary methods which are available to project the image on a screen.

"If this can be done successfully, then the objects imagined by a person would be clearly reflected on the screen as they are formed, and in this way every thought of the individual could be read. Our minds would then, indeed, be like open books."

Besides his discoveries concerning the harnessing of the new energy, television and thought photography, Mr. Tesla is working to produce a type of radio transmitter which will insure the strictest privacy in wireless communication regardless of the number of subscribers, and he is developing some important discoveries in molecular physics which will revolutionize the science of metallurgy and greatly improve metals.

After a discussion of his new scientific findings, Mr. Tesla turned to the subject of his personal source of energy and what he considers the real values of life. One of the most fundamental and also one of the saddest facts in human life is well brought out in a French proverb which, freely translated, means: "If youth had the knowledge and age the power of doing," said Mr. Tesla. "Our condition of body and mind in old age is merely a certificate of how we have spent our youth. The secret of my own strength and vitality today is that in my youth I led what you might call a virtuous life.

"I have never dissipated. When I was a young man I understood well the significance of that old French proverb, although I doubt that I had even heard it then. But I seemed to have a clear understanding while still young that I must control my passions and appetites if I wanted to make some of my dreams come true. So with this in view, quite early in life I set about disciplining myself, planning out a program of living for what I considered the sane and worthwhile life.

"Since I love my work above all things, it is only natural that I should wish to continue it until I die. I want no vacation, no surcease from my labor. If people would select a life work compatible with their temperaments, the sum total of happiness would be immeasurably increased in the world.

"Many are saddened and depressed by the brevity of life. 'What is the use of attempting to accomplish anything?' they say. 'Life is so short. We may never live to see the completion of the task.' Well, people could prolong their lives considerably if they would but make the effort. Human beings do so many things that pave the way to an early grave.

"First of all, we eat too much, but this we have heard said often before. And we eat the wrong kinds of foods and drink the wrong kind of liquids. Most of the harm is done by overeating and under exercising, which bring about toxic conditions in the body and make it impossible for the system to throw off the accumulated poisons.

"My regime for the good life and my diet? Well, for one thing, I drink plenty of milk and water. Why overburden the bodies that serve us? I eat but two meals a day, and I avoid all acid-producing foods. Almost everybody eats too many peas and beans and other foods containing uric acid and other poisons. I partake liberally of fresh vegetables, fish or meat sparingly, and rarely. Fish is reputed as fine brain food, but has a very strong acid reaction, as it contains a great deal of phosphorus. Acidity is by far the worst enemy to fight off in old age.

"Potatoes are splendid, and should be eaten at least once a day. They contain valuable mineral salts and are neutralizing. I believe in plenty of exercise. I walk eight or ten miles every day and never take a cab or other conveyances when I have the time to use leg power. I also exercise in my bath daily, for I think this is of great importance. I take a warm bath, followed by a prolonged cold shower.

"Sleep? I scarcely ever sleep. I come of a long-lived family, but it is noted for its poor sleepers. I expect to match the records of my ancestors and live to be at least 100. My sleeplessness does not worry me. Sometimes I doze for an hour or so. Occasionally, however, once in a few months, I may sleep for four or five hours. Then I awaken virtually charged with energy, like a battery. Nothing can stop me after such a night. I feel great strength then. There is no doubt about it but that sleep is a restorer, a vitalizer, that it increases energy. But on the other hand, I do not think it is essential to one's well being, particularly if one is habitually a poor sleeper.

"Today, at 77, as a result of well regulated life, sleeplessness notwithstanding, I have an excellent certificate of health. I never felt better in my life. I am energetic, strong, in full possession of all my mental faculties. In my prime I did not possess the energy I have today. And what is more, in solving my problems I use but a small part of the energy I possess, for I have learned how to conserve it. Because of my experiences and knowledge gained through the years, my tasks are much lighter. Contrary to general belief, work comes easier for older people if they are in good health, because they have learned through years of practice how to arrive at a given place by the shortest path."

TESLA'S "COSMIC ENDEAVORS"— HIS OWN STORY

IN very guarded words, Tesla once told of his ideas and thoughts of the afterlife, religion and what he referred to as the "Art of Telautomatics." We offer these wise words as proof that Tesla often thought in ways that escaped many other "great thinkers."

Ever since I was told by some of the greatest men of the time, leaders in science whose names are [a immortal, that I am possessed of an unusual mind, I bent all my thinking faculties on the solution of great problems regardless of sacrifice. For many years I endeavored to solve the enigma of death, and watched eagerly for every kind of spiritual indication. But only once in the course of my existence have I had an experience which momentarily impressed me as supernatural.

It was at the time of my mother's death. I had become completely exhausted by pain and long vigilance, and one night was carried to a building about two blocks from our home. As I lay helpless there, I thought that if my mother died while I was away from her bedside she would surely give me a sign.

Two or three months before I was in London in company with my late friend, Sir William Crookes, when spiritualism was discussed, and I was under the full sway of these thoughts. I might not have paid attention to other men, but was susceptible to his arguments, as it was his epochal work on radiant matter, which I had read as a student, that made me embrace the electrical career. I reflected that the conditions for a look into the beyond were most favorable, for my mother was a woman of genius and particularly excelling in the powers of intuition.

During the whole night, every fiber of my brain was stained in expectancy, but nothing happened until early in the morning, when I feel in a sleep, or perhaps a swoon, and saw a cloud carrying angelic figures of marvelous beauty, one of whom gazed upon me lovingly and gradually assumed the features of my mother. The appearance slowly floated across the room and vanished, and I was awakened by an indescribably sweet song of many voices. In that instant a certitude, which no words can express, came upon me that my mother had just died. And that was true. I was unable to understand the tremendous weight of the painful knowledge I receive in advance, and wrote a letter to Sir William Crookes while still under the domination of these impressions and in poor bodily health.

When I recovered I sought for a long time the external cause of this strange manifestation and, to my great relief, I succeeded after many months of fruitless effort. I had seen the painting of a celebrated artist, representing allegorically one of the seasons in the form of a cloud with a group of angels which seemed to actually float in the air, and this had struck me forcefully. It was exactly the same that appeared in my dream, with the exception of my mother's likeness. The music came from the choir in the church nearby at the early mass of Easter morning, explaining everything satisfactorily in conformity with scientific facts.

This occurred long ago, and I have never had the faintest reason since to change my views on psychic and spiritual phenomena, for which there is absolutely no foundation. The belief in these is the natural outgrowth of intellectual development.

Religious dogmas are no longer accepted in their orthodox meaning, but every individual clings to faith in a supreme power of some kind. We all must have an ideal to govern our conduct and insure contentment, but it is immaterial whether it be one of creed, art, science or anything else, so long as it fulfills the function of a dematerializing force.

It is essential to the peaceful existence of humanity as a whole that one common conception should prevail. While I have failed to obtain any evidence in support of the contentions of psychologists and spiritualists,

I have proved to my complete satisfaction that automatism of life, not only through continuous observations of individual actions, but even more conclusively through certain generalizations.

These amount to a discovery which I consider of the greatest moment to human society, and on which I shall briefly dwell. I got the first inkling of this astounding truth when I was still a very young man, but for many years In interpreted what I noted simply as coincidences.

Namely, whenever either myself or a person to whom I was attached, or a cause to which I was devoted, was hurt by others in a particular way, which might be best popularly characterized as the most unfair imaginable, I experienced a singular and undefinable pain which, for want of a better term, I have qualified as "cosmic," and shortly thereafter, and invariably, those who had inflicted it came to grief. After many such cases I confided this to a number of friends, who had the opportunity to convince themselves of the truth of the theory which I have gradually formulated and which may be stated in the following few words:

Our bodies are of similar construction and exposed to the same external influences. This results in likeness of response and concordance of the general activities on which all our social and other rules and laws are based. We are automata entirely controlled by the forces of the medium being tossed about like corks on the surface of the water, but mistaking the resultant of the impulses from the outside for free will. The movements and other actions we perform are always life preservative and though seemingly quite independent from one another, we are connected by invisible links.

So long as the organism is in perfect order it responds accurately to the agents that prompt it, but the moment that there is some derangement in any individual, his self-preservative power is impaired. Everybody understands, of course, that if one becomes deaf, has his eyesight weakened, or his limbs injured, the chances for his continued existence are lessened. But this is also true, and perhaps more so, of certain defects in the brain which deprive the automaton, more or less, of that vital quality and cause it to rush into destruction.

A very sensitive and observant being, with his highly developed mechanism all intact, and acting with precision in obedience to the changing conditions of the environment, is endowed with a transcending mechanical sense, enabling him to evade perils too subtle to be directly perceived. When he comes in contact with others whose controlling organs are radically faulty, that sense asserts itself and he feels the "cosmic" pain. The truth of this has been borne out in hundreds of instances and I am inviting other students of nature to devote attention to this subject, believing that through combined and systematic effort, results of incalculable value to the world will be attained.

The idea of constructing an automaton, to bear out my theory, presented itself to me early, but I did not begin active work until 1893, when I started my wireless investigations. During the succeeding two or three years a number of automatic mechanisms, to be actuated from a distance, were constructed by me and exhibited to visitors in my laboratory.

In 1896, however, I designed a complete machine capable of a multitude of operations, but the consummation of my labors was delayed until late in 1897. This machine was illustrated and described in my article in the *Century Magazine* of June, 1900, and other periodicals of that time and, when first shown in the beginning of 1898, it created a sensation such as no other invention of mine has ever produced. In November, 1898, a basic patent on the novel art was granted to me, but only after the

Examiner-in-Chief had come to New York and witnessed the performance, for which I claimed seem unbelievable. I remember that when later I called on an official in Washington, with a view of offering the invention to the Government, he burst out in laughter upon my telling him what I had accomplished. Nobody thought then that there was the faintest prospect of perfecting such a device. It is unfortunate that in this patent, following the advice of my attorneys, I indicated the control as being effected through the medium of a single circuit and a well-known form of detector, for the reason that I had not yet secured protection on my methods and apparatus for individualization. As a matter of fact, my boats were controlled through the joint action of several circuits and interference of every kind was excluded.

Most generally I employed receiving circuits in the form of loops, including condensers, because the discharges of my high-tension transmitter ionized the air in the hall, so that even a very small aerial would draw electricity from the surrounding atmosphere for hours.

Just to give an idea, I found, for instance, that a bulb 12" in diameter, highly exhausted, and with one single terminal to which a short wire was attached, would deliver well on to one thousand successive flashes before all charge of the air in the laboratory was neutralized. The loop form of receiver was not sensitive to such a disturbance and it is curious to note that it is becoming popular at this late date.

In reality, it collects much less energy than the aerials or a long grounded wire, but it so happens that it does away with a number of defects inherent to the present wireless devices. In demonstrating my invention before audiences, the visitors were requested to ask any questions, however involved, and the automaton would answer them by signs. This was considered magic at the time, but was I extremely simple, for it was myself who gave the replies by means of the device.

At the same period another larger telautomatic boat was constructed, a photograph of which is shown in this number of the *Electrical Experimenter*. It was controlled by loops, having several turns placed in the hull, which was made entirely water-tight and capable of submergence. The apparatus was similar to that used in the first with the exception of certain special features I introduced as, for example, incandescent lamps which afforded a visible evidence of the proper functioning of the machine.

These automata, controlled within the range of vision of the operator, were, however, the first and rather crude steps in the evolution of the Art of Telautomatics as I had conceived it. The next logical improvement was its application to automatic mechanisms beyond the limits of vision and at great distance from the center of control, and I have ever since advocated their employment as instruments of warfare in preference to guns. The importance of this now seems to be recognized, if I am to judge from casual announcements through the press of achievements which are said to be extraordinary, but contain no merit of novelty, whatever. In an imperfect manner it is practicable, with the existing wireless plants, to launch an aeroplane, have it follow a certain approximate course, and perform some operation at a distance of many hundreds of miles.

A machine of this kind can also be mechanically controlled in several ways and I have no doubt that it may prove of some usefulness in war. But there are, to my best knowledge, no instrumentalities in existence today with which such an object could be accomplished in a precise manner. I have devoted years of study to this matter and have evolved means, making such and greater wonders easily realizable.

As stated on a previous occasion, when I was a student at college I conceived a flying machine quite unlike the present ones. The underlying principle was sound but could not be carried into practice for want of a prime-mover of sufficiently great activity. In recent years, I have successfully solved the problem and am now planning aerial machines devoid of sustaining planes, ailerons, propellers and other external attachments, which will be capable of immense speeds and are very likely to furnish powerful arguments for peace in the near future.

Such a machine, sustained and propelled entirely by reaction, is shown at the end of this chapter, and is supposed to be controlled either mechanically or by wireless energy. By installing proper plants, it will be practicable to project a missile of this kind into the air and drop it almost on the very spot designated, which may be thousands of miles away. But we are not going to stop this. Telautomata will be ultimately produced, capable of acting as if possessed of their own intelligence, and their advent will create a revolution.

As early as 1898 I proposed to representatives of a large manufacturing concern the construction and public exhibition of an automobile carriage, which, left to itself, would perform a great variety of operations involving something akin to judgment. But my proposal was deemed chimerical at that time and nothing came from it.

At present, many of the ablest minds are trying to devise expedients for preventing a repetition of the awful conflict which is only theoretically ended and the duration and main issues of which I have correctly predicted in an article printed in the *Sun* of December 20, 1914. The proposed League is not a remedy but on the contrary, in the opinion of a number of competent men, may bring about results just the opposite. It is particularly regrettable that a punitive policy was adopted in framing the terms of peace, because a few years hence it will be possible for nations to fight without armies, ships or guns, by weapons far more terrible, to the destructive action and range of which there is virtually no limit.

A city, at any distance whatsoever from the enemy, can be destroyed by him and no power on earth can stop him from doing so. If we want to avert an impending calamity and a state of things which may transform this globe into an inferno, we should push the development of flying machines and wireless transmission of energy without an instant's delay and with all he power and resources of the nation.

TESLA'S CONCEPTION OF THE EARTH/ATMOSPHERE AS A GIANT ELECTRICAL CAPACITOR

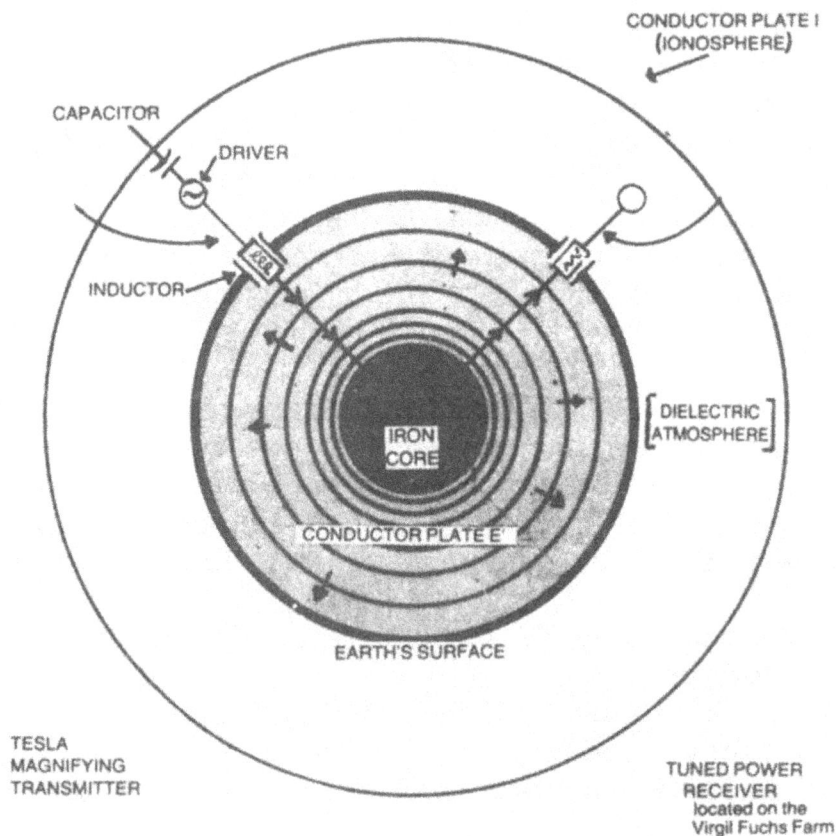

UFOs & ELECTROMAGNETISM

THERE are many who sincerely believe that Tesla was not of this realm. Some have taken his most secret work and tried to expand on it and develop technology that is truly not of this world. Unfortunately, Tesla is not around to give them a helping hand and so unfortunately, for the most part, these attempts to duplicate an alien technology have not been overly successful.

However, there is said to be in New Zealand a man who has built a flying saucer that can travel at incredible speeds. This vehicle is powered by a revolutionary motor harnessing natural energy from the atmosphere, much like what Tesla was known to be working on in seclusion shortly before his untimely death. This is an incredible project that was first written about in *The Star* of Auckland, New Zealand and it involves a British inventor and a group in New Zealand who are talking about financing him.

The machine would fly from Britain to Auckland in only 39 minutes. According to its New Zealand backers, a spectacular manned test flight is also planned within eight months if they can raise $20,000.

The craft, called a levity disc, is being designed by John Searl of Mortimer in Berkshire. He hopes to demonstrate it at the next Farnborough air show. Supporters say the levity disc could make rocketry obsolete, because it is:

* Noiseless and pollution-free.

* Requires no runways or launching pads for the vertical takeoff and landing.

* Does not need fuel as it has an "electromagnetic" motor with an energy force field built up to cushion it at supersonic speed.

Aucklander Veronica Comer is the spokesperson for the New Zealand section of Searl National Space Consortium. She told the *Star* this week John Searl and his helpers had made about 41 of the craft, varying in diameter from .9 to 11.5 meters, mostly unmanned, which had flown several hundred times around the world. Mrs. Comer claimed these flights were made secretly before 1971. "Many governments have shown interest in the Searl effect generator, and he has had the help of NASA in the United States and also the British government which put laboratory facilities at his disposal," she said. "He has just developed and [a patented a free energy generator for use in motor vehicles under special license..."

Mrs. Comer says Searl has a strong sense of destiny about his vertical disc invention. An engineer, he works around the clock to perfect his craft strenuously resisting huge monetary bids for his patents. On his drawing board, she says, is the design of a massive levity disc, code-named Starship Ezekiel, which he one day hopes to build for interplanetary flight.

Repeating Dream

Much like Tesla, John Searl was repeatedly plagued by the same terrifying dream when he was a boy. Later he came to realize this was an omen pointing him toward involvement in the realms of cosmic power and space flights. Searl's dreams revealed exactly how to construct his levity disc, says the Searl National Space Research Consortium's New Zealand spokesperson, Mrs. Veronica Comer.

Scientists scoffed at his layouts and designs. But undeterred, Searl pressed on to the state where he and his supporters firmly believe he'll force a major rethinking in science, magnetism and gravity.

Says Mrs. Comer: "This concept of technology opens a whole wide horizon which must only be for the betterment of the world in general."

And she claims that Searl effect EM energy is under study by the Royal Commission on nuclear power here in New Zealand. Searl has dedicated his life to bringing his new technology to the world. "All inventors suffer ridicule and opposition and Searl is no exception," says Mrs. Comer.

Searl's work has attracted newspaper publicity and television exposure in Britain, Germany, Japan and Australia, she adds. It's predicted John Searl will become famous for both his levity disc conception and universal use of his energy concepts.

The following excerpts have been taken from a letter and literature issue by the Consortium to supplement his *Star* article. "A number of physicists joined his team, including a well known professor from the Anti-Gravity Research Institute in Japan, whose technical book, ***Principles of Ultra Relativity***, referring in considerable detail to the Searl system was released throughout Japan. (Reuse of the Searl Effect Generator in motor vehicles: "This should be the forerunner of many such productions, for Free Energy can be used in every field where power or motivation is required, in the home, industry, shipping, mining, freight carrying and all methods of passenger travel. This source of power is inexhaustible and costs nothing.")

Searl's "flying saucers" have been secretly launched form a site near Warminster in England, probably giving rise to the UFO reports over a long period in that area. It does not erase the belief that we are being visited from outer space but increases the feasibility of interplanetary travel—for which perhaps we are being programmed.

STARSHIP EZEKIEL will take 2,000 persons, mainly scientists, geologists, astronomers and researchers, medical personnel, passengers and maintenance crew and staff. It will incorporate all the latest materials, components and technologies, will carry no fuel, and travel around the speed of light using Free Energy. The cost of constructing this craft will be approximately $24 million. It can stay aloft for two years, returning to Earth at intervals for supplies and change of crew.

Searl says that certain persons will stop at nothing to buy out, suppress or eliminate him if he becomes an opposition force on "their scene." He feels he is working under a spiritual cloak of protection as many times he has undergone attack, sabotage, including his family. He has been ridiculed, harangued, nearly driven into the ground both figuratively and literally (by car), but he carries on despite all odds.

Like Tesla, he could have been a rich man years ago if he had "given in" to the "system." When various governments would have put untold backing behind him for military research into his concept, but on each occasion he declined for he has utter conviction that this energy source is for the good and progression of mankind and not the destruction of it. For instance, the Arabs in 1973 offered $723 million for his prototype but he declined, feeling it would be used for an evil purpose (against Israel).

The Autobiography of Nikola Tesla

Chapter 1—Early Life

THE progressive development of man is vitally dependent on invention. It is the most important product of his creative brain. Its ultimate purpose is the complete mastery of mind over the material world, the harnessing of the forces of nature to human needs. This is the difficult task of the inventor who is often misunderstood and unrewarded. But he finds ample compensation in the pleasing exercises of his powers and in the knowledge of being one of that exceptionally privileged class without whom the race would have long ago perished in the bitter struggle against pitiless elements. Speaking for myself, I have already had more than my full measure of this exquisite enjoyment; so much, that for many years my life was little short of continuous rapture. I am credited with being one of the hardest workers and perhaps I am, if thought is the equivalent of labour, for I have devoted to it almost all of my waking hours. But if work is interpreted to be a definite performance in a specified time according to a rigid rule, then I may be the worst of idlers.

Every effort under compulsion demands a sacrifice of life-energy. I never paid such a price. On the contrary, I have thrived on my thoughts. In attempting to give a connected and faithful account of my activities in this story of my life, I must dwell, however reluctantly, on the impressions of my youth and the circumstances and events which have been instrumental in determining my career. Our first endeavors are purely instinctive prompting of an imagination vivid and undisciplined. As we grow older reason asserts itself and we become more and more systematic and designing. But those early impulses, though not immediately productive, are of the greatest moment and may shape our very destinies. Indeed, I feel now that had I understood and cultivated instead of suppressing them, I would have added substantial value to my bequest to the world.

But not until I had attained manhood did I realize that I was an inventor. This was due to a number of causes. In the first place, I had a brother who was gifted to an extraordinary degree; one of those rare phenomena of mentality which biological investigation has failed to explain. His premature death left my earth parents disconsolate. (I will explain my remark about my "earth parents" later.) We owned a horse which had been presented to us by a dear friend. It was a magnificent animal of Arabian breed, possessed of almost human intelligence, and was cared for and petted by the whole family, having on one occasion saved my dear father's life under remarkable circumstances.

My father had been called one winter night to perform an urgent duty and while crossing the mountains, infested by wolves, the horse became frightened and ran away, throwing him violently to the ground. It arrived home bleeding and exhausted, but after the alarm was sounded, immediately dashed off again, returning to the spot, and before the searching party were far on the way they were met by my father, who had recovered consciousness and remounted, not realizing that he had been lying in the snow for several hours. This horse was responsible for my brother's injuries from which he died. I witnessed the tragic scene and although so many years have elapsed since, my visual impression of it has lost none of its force. The recollection of his attainments made every effort of mine seem dull in comparison. Anything I did that was creditable merely caused my parents to feel their loss more keenly. So I grew up with little confidence in myself.

But I was far from being considered a stupid boy, if I am to judge from an incident of which I have still a strong remembrance. One day the Aldermen were passing through a street where I was playing with other boys. The oldest of these venerable gentlemen, a wealthy citizen, paused to give a silver piece to each of us. Coming to me, he suddenly stopped and commanded, "Look in my eyes." I met his gaze, my hand outstretched to receive the much valued coin, when to my dismay, he said, "No, not much; you can get nothing from me. You are too smart." They used to tell a funny story about me. I had two old aunts with wrinkled faces, one of them having two teeth protruding like the tusks of an elephant, which she buried in my cheek every time she kissed me. Nothing would scare me more then the prospects of being by these affectionate, unattractive relatives. It happened that while being carried in my mother's arms, they asked who was the prettier of the two. After examining their faces intently, I answered thoughtfully, pointing to one of them, "This here is not as ugly as the other."

Then again, I was intended from my very birth, for the clerical profession and this thought constantly oppressed me. I longed to be an engineer, but my father was inflexible. He was the son of an officer who served in the army of the Great Napoleon and in common with his brother, professor of mathematics in a prominent institution, had received a military education; but, singularly enough, later embraced the clergy in which vocation he achieved eminence. He was a very erudite man, a veritable natural philosopher, poet and writer and his sermons were said to be as eloquent as those of Abraham a-Sancta-Clara. He had a prodigious memory and frequently recited at length from works in several languages. He often remarked playfully that if some of the classics were lost he could restore them. His style of writing was much admired. He penned sentences short and terse and full of wit and satire. The humorous remarks he made were always peculiar and characteristic. Just to illustrate, I may mention one or two instances. Among the help, there was a cross-eyed man called Mane, employed to do work around the farm. He was chopping wood one day. As he swung the axe, my father, who stood nearby and felt very uncomfortable, cautioned him, "For God's sake, Mane, do not strike at what you are looking but at what you intend to hit."

On another occasion, he was taking out for a drive, a friend who carelessly permitted his costly fur coat to rub on the carriage wheel. My father reminded him of it saying, "Pull in your coat; you are ruining my tire." He had the odd habit of talking to himself and would often carry on an animated conversation and indulge in heated argument, changing the tone of his voice. A casual listener might have sworn that several people were in the room. Although I must trace to my mother's influence whatever inventiveness I possess, the training he gave me must have been helpful. It comprised all sorts of exercises - as, guessing one another's thoughts, discovering the defects of some form of expression, repeating long sentences or performing mental calculations. These daily lessons were intended to strengthen memory and reason, and especially to develop the critical sense, and were undoubtedly very beneficial. My mother descended from one of the oldest families in the country and a line of inventors. Both her father and grandfather originated numerous implements for household, agricultural and other uses. She was a truly great woman, of rare skill, courage and fortitude, who had braved the storms of life and passed through many a trying experience. When she was sixteen, a virulent pestilence swept the country. Her father was called away to administer the last sacraments to the dying and during his absence she went alone to the assistance of a neighboring family who were stricken by the dread disease. She bathed, clothed and laid out the bodies, decorating them with flowers according to the custom of the country and when her father returned he found everything ready for a Christian burial.

My mother was an inventor of the first order and would, I believe, have achieved great things had she not been so remote from modern life and its multi fold opportunities. She invented and constructed all kinds of tools and devices and wove the finest designs from thread which was spun by her. She even planted seeds, raised the plants and separated the fibbers herself. She worked indefatigably, from break of day till late at night, and most of the wearing apparel and furnishings of the home were the product of her hands. When she was past sixty, her fingers were still nimble enough to tie three knots in an eyelash. There was another and still more important reason for my late awakening. In my boyhood, I suffered from a peculiar affliction due to the appearance of images, often accompanied by strong flashes of light, which marred the sight of real objects and interfered with my thoughts and action. They were pictures of things and scenes which I had really seen, never of those imagined. When a word was spoken to me the image of the object it designated would present itself vividly to my vision and sometimes I was quite unable to distinguish weather what I saw was tangible or not. This caused me great discomfort and anxiety. None of the students of psychology or physiology whom I have consulted, could ever explain satisfactorily these phenomenon. They seem to have been unique although I was probably predisposed as I know that my brother experienced a similar trouble. The theory I have formulated is that the images were the result of a reflex action from the brain on the retina under great excitation. They certainly were not hallucinations such as are produced in diseased and anguished minds, for in other respects I was normal and composed. To give an idea of my distress, suppose that I had witnessed a funeral or some such nerve-wracking spectacle. The, inevitably, in the stillness of night, a vivid picture of the scene would thrust itself before my eyes and persist despite all my efforts to banish it. If my explanation is correct, it should be possible to project on a screen the image of any object one conceives and make it visible. Such an advance would revolutionize all human relations. I am convinced that this wonder can and will be accomplished in time to come. I may add that I have devoted much thought to the solution of the problem.

I have managed to reflect such a picture, which I have seen in my mind, to the mind of another person, in another room. To free myself of these tormenting appearances, I tried to concentrate my mind on something else I had seen, and in this way I would often obtain temporary relief; but in order to get it I had to conjure continuously new images. It was not long before I found that I had exhausted all of those at my command; my 'reel' had run out as it were, because I had seen little of the world – only objects in my home and the immediate surroundings. As I performed these mental operations for the second or third time, in order to chase the appearances from my vision, the remedy gradually lost all its force. Then I instinctively commenced to make excursions beyond the limits of the small world of which I had knowledge, and I saw new scenes. These were at first very blurred and indistinct, and would flit away when I tried to concentrate my attention upon them. They gained in strength and distinctness and finally assumed the concreteness of real things. I soon discovered that my best comfort was attained if I simply went on in my vision further and further, getting new impressions all the time, and so I began to travel; of course, in my mind. Every night, (and sometimes during the day), when alone, I would start on my journeys – see new places, cities and countries; live there, meet people and make friendships and acquaintances and, however unbelievable, it is a fact that they were just as dear to me as those in actual life, and not a bit less intense in their manifestations. This I did constantly until I was about seventeen, when my thoughts turned seriously to invention. Then I observed to my delight that I could visualize with the greatest facility. I needed no models, drawings or experiments. I could picture them all as real in my mind. Thus I have been led unconsciously to evolve what I consider a new method of materializing inventive concepts and ideas, which is radially opposite to the purely experimental and is in my opinion ever so much more expeditious and efficient.

The moment one constructs a device to carry into practice a crude idea, he finds himself unavoidably engrossed with the details of the apparatus. As he goes on improving and reconstructing, his force of concentration diminishes and he loses sight of the great underlying principle. Results may be obtained, but always at the sacrifice of quality. My method is different. I do not rush into actual work. When I get an idea, I start at once building it up in my imagination. I change the construction, make improvements and operate the device in my mind. It is absolutely immaterial to me whether I run my turbine in thought or test it in my shop. I even note if it is out of balance. There is no difference whatever; the results are the same. In this way I am able to rapidly develop and perfect a conception without touching anything. When I have gone so far as to embody in the invention every possible improvement I can think of and see no fault anywhere, I put into concrete form this final product of my brain. Invariably my device works as I conceived that it should, and the experiment comes out exactly as I planned it. In twenty years there has not been a single exception. Why should it be otherwise? Engineering, electrical and mechanical, is positive in results. There is scarcely a subject that cannot be examined beforehand, from the available theoretical and practical data. The carrying out into practice of a crude idea as is being generally done, is, I hold, nothing but a waste of energy, money, and time.

My early affliction had however, another compensation. The incessant mental exertion developed my powers of observation and enabled me to discover a truth of great importance. I had noted that the appearance of images was always preceded by actual vision of scenes under peculiar and generally very exceptional conditions, and I was impelled on each occasion to locate the original impulse. After a while this effort grew to be almost automatic and I gained great facility in connecting cause and effect. Soon I became aware, to my surprise, that every thought I conceived was suggested by an external impression. Not only this but all my actions were prompted in a similar way. In the course of time it became perfectly evident to me that I was merely an automation endowed with power of movement responding to the stimuli of the sense organs and thinking and acting accordingly. The practical result of this was the art of teleautomatics which has been so far carried out only in an imperfect manner. Its latent possibilities will, however be eventually shown. I have been years planning self-controlled automata and believe that mechanisms can be produced which will act as if possessed of reason, to a limited degree, and will create a revolution in many commercial and industrial departments. I was about twelve years of age when I first succeeded in banishing an image from my vision by willful effort, but I never had any control over the flashes of light to which I have referred. They were, perhaps, my strangest and [most] inexplicable experience. They usually occurred when I found myself in a dangerous or distressing situations or when I was greatly exhilarated. In some instances I have seen all the air around me filled with tongues of living flame. Their intensity, instead of diminishing, increased with time and seemingly attained a maximum when I was about twenty-five years old.

While in Paris in 1883, a prominent French manufacturer sent me an invitation to a shooting expedition which I accepted. I had been long confined to the factory and the fresh air had a wonderfully invigorating effect on me. On my return to the city that night, I felt a positive sensation that my brain had caught fire. I was a light as though a small sun was located in it and I passed the whole night applying cold compresses to my tortured head. Finally the flashes diminished in frequency and force but it took more than three weeks before they wholly subsided. When a second invitation was extended to me, my answer was an emphatic NO!

These luminous phenomena still manifest themselves from time to time, as when a new idea opening up possibilities strikes me, but they are no longer exciting, being of relatively small intensity. When I close my eyes I invariably observe first, a background of very dark and uniform blue, not unlike the sky on a clear but starless night. In a few seconds this field becomes animated with innumerable scintillating flakes of green, arranged in several layers and advancing towards me. Then there appears, to the right, a beautiful pattern of two systems of parallel and closely spaced lines, at right angles to one another, in all sorts of colors with yellow, green, and gold predominating. Immediately thereafter, the lines grow brighter and the whole is thickly sprinkled with dots of twinkling light. This picture moves slowly across the field of vision and in about ten seconds vanishes on the left, leaving behind a ground of rather unpleasant and inert grey until the second phase is reached. Every time, before falling asleep, images of persons or objects flit before my view. When I see them I know I am about to lose consciousness. If they are absent and refuse to come, it means a sleepless night. To what an extent imagination played in my early life, I may illustrate by another odd experience.

Like most children, I was fond of jumping and developed an intense desire to support myself in the air. Occasionally a strong wind richly charged with oxygen blew from the mountains, rendering my body light as cork and then I would leap and float in space for a long time. It was a delightful sensation and my disappointment was keen when later I undeceived myself. During that period I contracted many strange likes, dislikes and habits, some of which I can trace to external impressions while others are unaccountable. I had a violent aversion against the earrings of women, but other ornaments, as bracelets, pleased me more or less according to design. The sight of a pearl would almost give me a fit, but I was fascinated with the glitter of crystals or objects with sharp edges and plane surfaces. I would not touch the hair of other people except, perhaps at the point of a revolver. I would get a fever by looking at a peach and if a piece of camphor was anywhere in the house it caused me the keenest discomfort. Even now I am not insensible to some of these upsetting impulses. When I drop little squares of paper in a dish filled with liquid, I always sense a peculiar and awful taste in my mouth. I counted the steps in my walks and calculated the cubical contents of soup plates, coffee cups and pieces of food, otherwise my meal was unenjoyable. All repeated acts or operations I performed had to be divisible by three and if I missed I felt impelled to do it all over again, even if it took hours. Up to the age of eight years, my character was weak and vacillating. I had neither courage or strength to form a firm resolve. My feelings came in waves and surges and variated unceasingly between extremes. My wishes were of consuming force and like the heads of the hydra, they multiplied. I was oppressed by thoughts of pain in life and death and religious fear. I was swayed by superstitious belief and lived in constant dread of the spirit of evil, of ghosts and ogres and other unholy monsters of the dark. Then all at once, there came a tremendous change which altered the course of my whole existence.

Of all things I liked books best. My father had a large library and whenever I could manage I tried to satisfy my passion for reading. He did not permit it and would fly in a rage when he caught me in the act. He hid the candles when he found that I was reading in secret. He did not want me to spoil my eyes. But I obtained tallow, made the wicking and cast the sticks into tin forms, and every night I would bush the keyhole and the cracks and read, often till dawn, when all others slept and my mother started on her arduous daily tasks. On one occasion I came across a novel entitled '*Aoafi*,' (the son of Aba), a Serbian translation of a well known Hungarian writer, Josika. This work somehow awakened my dormant powers of will and I began to practice self-control. At first my resolutions faded like snow in April, but in a little while I conquered my weakness and felt a pleasure I never knew before -- that of doing as I willed.

In the course of time this vigorous mental exercise became second to nature. At the outset my wishes had to be subdued but gradually desire and will grew to be identical. After years of such discipline I gained so complete a mastery over myself that I toyed with passions which have meant destruction to some of the strongest men. At a certain age I contracted a mania for gambling which greatly worried my parents. To sit down to a game of cards was for me the quintessence of pleasure. My father led an exemplary life and could not excuse the senseless waste of my time and money in which I indulged. I had a strong resolve, but my philosophy was bad. I would say to him, 'I can stop whenever I please, but it it worth while to give up that which I would purchase with the joys of paradise?' On frequent occasions he gave vent to his anger and contempt, but my mother was different. She understood the character of men and knew that one's salvation could only be brought about through his own efforts. One afternoon,

I remember, when I had lost all my money and was craving for a game, she came to me with a roll of bills and said, 'Go and enjoy yourself. The sooner you lose all we possess, the better it will be. I know that you will get over it.' She was right. I conquered my passion then and there and only regretted that it had not been a hundred times as strong. I not only vanquished but tore it from my heart so as not to leave even a trace of desire. Ever since that time I have been as indifferent to any form of gambling as to picking teeth. During another period I smoked excessively, threatening to ruin my health. Then my will asserted itself and I not only stopped but destroyed all inclination. Long ago I suffered from heart trouble until I discovered that it was due to the innocent cup of coffee I consumed every morning. I discontinued at once, though I confess it was not an easy task. In this way I checked and bridled other habits and passions, and have not only preserved my life but derived an immense amount of satisfaction from what most men would consider privation and sacrifice. After finishing the studies at the Polytechnic Institute and University, I had a complete nervous breakdown and while the malady lasted I observed many phenomena, strange and unbelievable...

Chapter 2—Extraordinary Experiences

I shall dwell briefly on these extraordinary experiences, on account of their possible interest to students of psychology and physiology and also because this period of agony was of the greatest consequence on my mental development and subsequent labors. But it is indispensable to first relate the circumstances and conditions which preceded them and in which might be found their partial explanation. From childhood I was compelled to concentrate attention upon myself. This caused me much suffering, but to my present view, it was a blessing in disguise for it has taught me to appreciate the inestimable value of introspection in the preservation of life, as well as a means of achievement. The pressure of occupation and the incessant stream of impressions pouring into our consciousness through all the gateways of knowledge make modern existence hazardous in many ways. Most persons are so absorbed in the contemplation of the outside world that they are wholly oblivious to what is passing on within themselves. The premature death of millions is primarily traceable to this cause. Even among those who exercise care, it is a common mistake to avoid imaginary, and ignore the real dangers. And what is true of an individual also applies, more or less, to a people as a whole.

Abstinence was not always to my liking, but I find ample reward in the agreeable experiences I am now making. Just in the hope of converting some to my precepts and convictions I will recall one or two. A short time ago I was returning to my hotel. It was a bitter cold night, the ground slippery, and no taxi to be had. Half a block behind me followed another man, evidently as anxious as myself to get under cover. Suddenly my legs went up in the air. At the same instant there was a flash in my brain. The nerves responded, the muscles contracted. I swung 180 degrees and landed on my hands. I resumed my walk as though nothing had happened when the stranger caught up with me. "How old are you?" he asked, surveying me critically. "Oh, about fifty-nine," I replied, "What of it?" "Well," said he, "I have seen a cat do this but never a man." About a month ago I wanted to order new eyeglasses and went to an oculist who put me through the usual tests. He looked at me incredulously as I read off with ease the smallest print at considerable distance. But when I told him I was past sixty he gasped in astonishment. Friends of mine often remark that my suits fit me like gloves but they do not know that all my clothing is made to measurements which were taken nearly fifteen years ago and never changed. During this same period my weight has not varied one pound. In this connection I may tell a funny story.

One evening, in the winter of 1885, Mr. Edison, Edward H. Johnson, the President of the Edison Illuminating Company, Mr. Bachelor, Manager of the works, and myself, entered a little place opposite 65 Firth Avenue, where the offices of the company were located. Someone suggested guessing weights and I was induced to step on a scale. Edison felt me all over and said: "Tesla weighs 152 lbs. to an ounce," and he guessed it exactly. Stripped I weighed 142 pounds, and that is still my weight. I whispered to Mr. Johnson; "How is it possible that Edison could guess my weight so closely?" "Well," he said, lowering his voice. "I will tell you confidentially, but you must not say anything. He was employed for a long time in a Chicago slaughter- house where he weighed thousands of hogs every day. That's why."

My friend, the Hon. Chauncey M. Dupew, tells of an Englishman on whom he sprung one of his original anecdotes and who listened with a puzzled expression, but a year later, laughed out loud. I will frankly confess it took me longer than that to appreciate Johnson's joke. Now, my well-being is simply the result of a careful and measured mode of living and perhaps the most astonishing thing is that three times in my youth I was rendered by illness a hopeless physical wreck and given up by physicians. MORE than this, through ignorance and lightheartedness, I got into all sorts of difficulties, dangers and scrapes from which I extricated myself as by enchantment. I was almost drowned, entombed, lost and frozen. I had hairbreadth escapes from mad dogs, hogs, and other wild animals. I passed through dreadful diseases and met with all kinds of odd mishaps and that I am whole and hearty today seems like a miracle. But as I recall these incidents to my mind I feel convinced that my preservation was not altogether accidental, but was indeed the work of divine power. An inventor's endeavor is essentially life saving. Whether he harnesses forces, improves devices, or provides new comforts and conveniences, he is adding to the safety of our existence. He is also better qualified than the average individual to protect himself in peril, for he is observant and resourceful. If I had no other evidence that I was, in a measure, possessed of such qualities, I would find it in these personal experiences. The reader will be able to judge for himself if I mention one or two instances. On one occasion, when about fourteen years old, I wanted to scare some friends who were bathing with me. My plan was to dive under a long floating structure and slip out quietly at the other end. Swimming and diving came to me as naturally as to a duck and I was confident that I could perform the feat. Accordingly I plunged into the water and, when out of view, turned around and proceeded rapidly towards the opposite side. Thinking that I was safely beyond the structure, I rose to the surface but to my dismay struck a beam. Of course, I quickly dived and forged ahead with rapid strokes until my breath was beginning to give out. Rising for the second time, my head came again in contact with a beam. Now I was becoming desperate. However, summoning all my energy, I made a third frantic attempt but the result was the same. The torture of suppressed breathing was getting unendurable, my brain was reeling and I felt myself sinking. At that moment, when my situation seemed absolutely hopeless, I experienced one of those flashes of light and the structure above me appeared before my vision. I either discerned or guessed that there was a little space between the surface of the water and the boards resting on the beams and, with consciousness nearly gone, I floated up, pressed my mouth close to the planks and managed to inhale a little air, unfortunately mingled with a spray of water which nearly choked me. Several times I repeated this procedure as in a dream until my heart, which was racing at a terrible rate, quieted down, and I gained composure. After that I made a number of unsuccessful dives, having completely lost the sense of direction, but finally succeeded in getting out of the trap when my friends had already given me up and were fishing for my body. That bathing season was spoiled for me through recklessness but I soon forgot the lesson and only two years later I fell into a worse predicament.

There was a large flourmill with a dam across the river near the city where I was studying at the time. As a rule the height of the water was only two or three inches above the dam and to swim to it was a sport not very dangerous in which I often indulged. One day I went alone to the river to enjoy myself as usual. When I was a short distance from the masonry, however, I was horrified to observe that the water had risen and was carrying me along swiftly. I tried to get away but it was too late. Luckily, though, I saved myself from being swept over by taking hold of the wall with both hands. The pressure against my chest was great and I was barely able to keep my head above the surface. Not a soul was in sight and my voice was lost in the roar of the fall. Slowly and gradually I became exhausted and unable to withstand the strain longer. Just as I was about to let go, to be dashed against the rocks below, I saw in a flash of light a familiar diagram illustrating the hydraulic principle that the pressure of a fluid in motion is proportionate to the area exposed and automatically I turned on my left side. As if by magic, the pressure was reduced and I found it comparatively easy in that position to resist the force of the stream. But the danger still confronted me. I knew that sooner or later I would be carried down, as it was not possible for any help to reach me in time, even if I had attracted attention. I am ambidextrous now, but then I was left-handed and had comparatively little strength in my right arm. For this reason I did not dare to turn on the other side to rest and nothing remained but to slowly push my body along the dam. I had to get away from the mill towards which my face was turned, as the current there was much swifter and deeper. It was a long and painful ordeal and I came near to failing at its very end, for I was confronted with a depression in the masonry. I managed to get over with the last ounce of my strength and fell in a swoon when I reached the bank, where I was found. I had torn virtually all the skin from my left side and it took several weeks before the fever had subsided and I was well. These are only two of many instanced, but they may be sufficient to show that had it not been for the inventor's instinct, I would not have lived to tell the tale.

Interested people have often asked me how and when I began to invent. This I can only answer from my present recollection in the light of which, the first attempt I recall was rather ambitious for it involved the invention of an apparatus and a method. In the former I was anticipated, but the later was original. It happened in this way. One of my playmates had come into the possession of a hook and fishing tackle which created quite an excitement in the village, and the next morning all started out to catch frogs. I was left alone and deserted owing to a quarrel with this boy. I had never seen a real hook and pictured it as something wonderful, endowed with peculiar qualities, and was despairing not to be one of the party. Urged by necessity, I somehow got hold of a piece of soft iron wire, hammered the end to a sharp point between two stones, bent it into shape, and fastened it to a strong string. I then cut a rod, gathered some bait, and went down to the brook where there were frogs in abundance. But I could not catch any and was almost discouraged when it occurred to me dangle the empty hook in front of a frog sitting on a stump. At first he collapsed but by and by his eyes bulged out and became bloodshot, he swelled to twice his normal size and made a vicious snap at the hook. Immediately I pulled him up. I tried the same thing again and again and the method proved infallible. When my comrades, who in spite of their fine outfit had caught nothing, came to me, they were green with envy. For a long time I kept my secret and enjoyed the monopoly but finally yielded to the spirit of Christmas. Every boy could then do the same and the following summer brought disaster to the frogs.

In my next attempt, I seem to have acted under the first instinctive impulse which later dominated me, -- to harness the energies of nature to the service of man. I did this through the medium of May bugs, or June bugs as they are called in America, which were a veritable pest in that country and sometimes broke the branches of trees by the sheer weight of their bodies. The bushes were black with them. I would attach as many as four of them to a crosspiece, rotably arranged on a thin spindle, and transmit the motion of the same to a large disc and so derive considerable 'power.' These creatures were remarkably efficient, for once they were started, they had no sense to stop and continued whirling for hours and hours and the hotter it was, the harder they worked. All went well until a strange boy came to the place. He was the son of a retired officer in the Austrian army. That urchin ate Maybugs alive and enjoyed them as though they were the finest blue-point oysters. That disgusting sight terminated my endeavors in this promising field and I have never since been able to touch a Maybug or any other insect for that matter.

After that, I believe, I undertook to take apart and assemble the clocks of my grandfather. In the former operation I was always successful, but often failed in the latter. So it came that he brought my work to a sudden halt in a manner not too delicate and it took thirty years before I tackled another clockwork again.

Shortly thereafter, I went into the manufacture of a kind of popgun which comprised a hollow tube, a piston, and two plugs of hemp. When firing the gun, the piston was pressed against the stomach and the tube was pushed back quickly with both hands. The air between the plugs was compressed and raised to a high temperature and one of them was expelled with a loud report. The art consisted in selecting a tube of the proper taper from the hollow stalks which were found in our garden. I did very well with that gun, but my activities interfered with the window panes in our house and met with painful discouragement.

If I remember rightly, I then took to carving swords from pieces of furniture which I could conveniently obtain. At that time I was under the sway of the Serbian national poetry and full of admiration for the feats of the heroes. I used to spend hours in mowing down my enemies in the form of cornstalks which ruined the crops and netted me several spankings from my mother.

Moreover, these were not of the formal kind but the genuine article. I had all this and more behind me before I was six years old and had passed through one year of elementary school in the village of Smiljan where my family lived. At this juncture we moved to the little city of Gospic nearby. This change of residence was like a calamity to me. It almost broke my heart to part from our pigeons, chickens and sheep, and our magnificent flock of geese which used to rise to the clouds in the morning and return from the feeding grounds at sundown in battle formation, so perfect that it would have put a squadron of the best aviators of the present day to shame. In our new house I was but a prisoner, watching the strange people I saw through my window blinds. My bashfulness was such that I would rather have faced a roaring lion than one of the city dudes who strolled about. But my hardest trial came on Sunday when I had to dress up and attend the service. There I met with an accident, the mere thought of which made my blood curdle like sour milk for years afterwards. It was my second adventure in a church. Not long before, I was entombed for a night in an old chapel on an inaccessible mountain which was visited only once a year. It was an awful experience, but this one was worse.

There was a wealthy lady in town, a good but pompous woman, who used to come to the church gorgeously painted up and attired with an enormous train and attendants. One Sunday I had just finished ringing the bell in the belfry and rushed downstairs, when this grand dame was sweeping out and I jumped on her train. It tore off with a ripping noise which sounded like a salvo of musketry fired by raw recruits. My father was livid with rage. He gave me a gentle slap on the cheek, the only corporal punishment he ever administered to me, but I almost feel it now. The embarrassment and confusion that followed are indescribably. I was practically ostracized until something else happened which redeemed me in the estimation of the community.

An enterprising young merchant had organized a fire department. A new fire engine was purchased, uniforms provided and the men drilled for service and parade. The engine was beautifully painted red and black. One afternoon, the official trial was prepared for and the machine was transported to the river. The entire population turned out to witness the great spectacle. When all the speeches and ceremonies were concluded, the command was given to pump, but not a drop of water came from the nozzle. The professors and experts tried in vain to locate the trouble. The fizzle was complete when I arrived at the scene. My knowledge of the mechanism was nil and I knew next to nothing of air pressure, but instinctively I felt for the suction hose in the water and found that it had collapsed. When I waded in the river and opened it up, the water rushed forth and not a few Sunday clothes were spoiled. Archimedes running naked through the streets of Syracuse and shouting Eureka at the top of his voice did not make a greater impression than myself. I was carried on the shoulders and was hero of the day.

Upon settling in the city I began a four years course in the so-called Normal School preparatory to my studies at the College or Real-Gymnasium. During this period my boyish efforts and exploits as well as troubles, continued. Among other things, I attained the unique distinction of champion crow catcher in the country. My method of procedure was extremely simple. I would go into the forest, hide in the bushes, and imitate the call of the birds. Usually I would get several answers and in a short while a crow would flutter down into the shrubbery near me. After that, all I needed to do was to throw a piece of cardboard to detract its attention, jump up and grab it before it could extricate itself from the undergrowth. In this way I would capture as many as I desired. But on one occasion something occurred which made me respect them. I had caught a fine pair of birds and was returning home with a friend. When we left the forest, thousands of crows had gathered making a frightful racket. In a few minutes they rose in pursuit and soon enveloped us. The fun lasted until all of a sudden I received a blow on the back of my head which knocked me down. Then they attacked me viciously. I was compelled to release the two birds and was glad to join my friend who had taken refuge in a cave.

In the schoolroom there were a few mechanical models which interested me and turned my attention to water turbines. I constructed many of these and found great pleasure in operating them. How extraordinary was my life an incident may illustrate. My uncle had no use for this kind of pastime and more than once rebuked me. I was fascinated by a description of Niagara Falls I had perused, and pictured in my imagination a big wheel run by the falls. I told my uncle that I would go to America and carry out this scheme. Thirty years later I was my ideas carried out at Niagara and marveled at the unfathomable mystery of the mind. I made all kinds of other contrivances and contraptions but among those, the arbalests I produced were the best. My arrows, when short, disappeared from sight and at close range traversed a plank of pine one inch thick. Through the continuous tightening of the bows I developed a skin on my stomach much like that of a crocodile and I am often wondering whether it is due to this exercise that I am able even now to digest cobblestones! Nor can I pass in silence my performances with the sling which would have enabled me to give a stunning exhibit at the Hippodrome. And now I will tell of one of my feats with this unique implement of war which will strain to the utmost the credulity of the reader.

I was practicing while walking with my uncle along the river. The sun was setting, the trout were playful and from time to time one would shoot up into the air, its glistening body sharply defined against a projecting rock beyond. Of course any boy might have hit a fish under these propitious conditions but I undertook a much more difficult task and I foretold to my uncle, to the minutest detail, what I intended doing. I was to hurl a stone to meet the fish, press its body against the rock, and cut it in two. It was no sooner said than done. My uncle looked at me almost scared out of his wits and exclaimed "Vade retra Satanae!" and it was a few days before he spoke to me again. Other records, however great, will be eclipsed but I feel that I could peacefully rest on my laurels for a thousand years.

Chapter 3—The Rotary Magnetic Field

AT the age of ten I entered the Real gymnasium which was a new and fairly well equipped institution. In the department of physics were various models of classical scientific apparatus, electrical and mechanical. The demonstrations and experiments performed from time to time by the instructors fascinated me and were undoubtedly a powerful incentive to invention. I was also passionately fond of mathematical studies and often won the professor's praise for rapid calculation. This was due to my acquired facility of visualizing the figures and performing the operation, not in the usual intuitive manner, but as in actual life. Up to a certain degree of complexity it was absolutely the same to me whether I wrote the symbols on the board or conjured them before my mental vision. But freehand drawing, to which many hours of the course were devoted, was an annoyance I could not endure. This was rather remarkable as most of the members of the family excelled in it. Perhaps my aversion was simply due to the predilection I found in undisturbed thought. Had it not been for a few exceptionally stupid boys, who could not do anything at all, my record would have been the worst.

It was a serious handicap as under the then existing educational regime drawing being obligatory, this deficiency threatened to spoil my whole career and my father had considerable trouble in railroading me from one class to another. In the second year at that institution I became obsessed with the idea of producing continuous motion through steady air pressure. The pump incident, of which I have been told, had set afire my youthful imagination and impressed me with the boundless possibilities of a vacuum. I grew frantic in my desire to harness this inexhaustible energy but for a long time I was groping in the dark. Finally, however, my endeavors crystallized in an invention which was to enable me to achieve what no other mortal ever attempted. Imagine a cylinder freely rotatable on two bearings and partly surrounded by a rectangular trough which fits it perfectly. The open side of the trough is enclosed by a partition so that the cylindrical segment within the enclosure divides the latter into two compartments entirely separated from each other by airtight sliding joints. One of these compartments being sealed and once for all exhausted, the other remaining open, a perpetual rotation of the cylinder would result. At least, so I thought.

A wooden model was constructed and fitted with infinite care and when I applied the pump on one side and actual observed that there was a tendency to turning, I was delirious with joy. Mechanical flight was the one thing I wanted to accomplish although still under the discouraging recollection of a bad fall I sustained by jumping with an umbrella from the top of a building. Every day I used to transport myself through the air to distant regions but could not understand just how I managed to do it. Now I had something concrete, a flying machine with nothing more than a rotating shaft, flapping wings, and; - a vacuum of unlimited power! From that time on I made my daily aerial excursions in a vehicle of comfort and luxury as might have befitted King Solomon. It took years before I understood that the atmospheric pressure acted at right angles to the surface of the cylinder and that the slight rotary effort I observed was due to a leak! Though this knowledge came gradually it gave me a painful shock. I had hardly completed my course at the Real Gymnasium when I was prostrated with a dangerous illness or rather, a score of them, and my condition became so desperate that I was given up by physicians. During this period I was permitted to read constantly, obtaining books from the Public Library which had been neglected and entrusted to me for classification of the works and preparation of catalogues.

One day I was handed a few volumes of new literature unlike anything I had ever read before and so captivating as to make me utterly forget me hopeless state. They were the earlier works of Mark Twain and to them might have been due the miraculous recovery which followed. Twenty-five years later, when I met Mr. Clemens and we formed a friendship between us, I told him of the experience and was amazed to see that great man of laughter burst into tears... My studies were continued at the higher Real Gymnasium in Carlstadt, Croatia, where one of my aunts resided. She was a distinguished lady, the wife of a Colonel who was an old war-horse having participated in many battles, I can never forget the three years I passed at their home. No fortress in time of war was under a more rigid discipline. I was fed like a canary bird. All the meals were of the highest quality and deliciously prepared, but short in quantity by a thousand percent. The slices of ham cut by my aunt were like tissue paper. When the Colonel would put something substantial on my plate she would snatch it away and say excitedly to him, "Be careful. Niko is very delicate." I had a voracious appetite and suffered like Tantalus. But I lived in an atmosphere of refinement and artistic taste quite unusual for those times and conditions. The land was low and marshy and malaria fever never left me while there despite the enormous amounts of quinine I consumed. Occasionally the river would rise and drive an army of rats into the buildings, devouring everything, even to the bundles of fierce paprika. These pests were to me a welcome diversion. I thinned their ranks by all sorts of means, which won me the unenviable distinction of rat-catcher in the community. At last, however, my course was completed, the misery ended, and I obtained the certificate of maturity which brought me to the crossroads.

During all those years my parents never wavered in their resolve to make me embrace the clergy, the mere thought of which filled me with dread. I had become intensely interested in electricity under the stimulating influence of my Professor of Physics, who was an ingenious man and often demonstrated the principles by apparatus of his own invention. Among these I recall a device in the shape of a freely rotatable bulb, with tinfoil coating, which was made to spin rapidly when connected to a static machine. It is impossible for me to convey an adequate idea of the intensity of feeling I experienced in witnessing his exhibitions of these mysterious phenomena. Every impression produced a thousand echoes in my mind. I wanted to know more of this wonderful force; I longed for experiment and investigation and resigned myself to the inevitable with aching heart. Just as I was making ready for the long journey home I received word that my father wished me to go on a shooting expedition. It was a strange request as he had been always strenuously opposed to this kind of sport. But a few days later I learned that the cholera was raging in that district and, taking advantage of an opportunity, I returned to Gospic in disregard to my parent's wishes. It is incredible how absolutely ignorant people were as to the causes of this scourge which visited the country in intervals of fifteen to twenty years. They thought that the deadly agents were transmitted through the air and filled it with pungent odors and smoke. In the meantime they drank infested water and died in heaps. I contracted the dreadful disease on the very day of my arrival and although surviving the crisis, I was confined to bed for nine months with scarcely any ability to move. My energy was completely exhausted and for the second time I found myself at Death's door.

In one of the sinking spells which was thought to be the last, my father rushed into the room. I still see his pallid face as he tried to cheer me in tones belying his assurance. "Perhaps," I said, "I may get well if you will let me study engineering." "You will go to the best technical institution in the world," he solemnly replied, and I knew that he meant it. A heavy weight was lifted from my mind but the relief would have come too late had it not been for a marvelous cure brought through a bitter decoction of a peculiar bean. I came to life like Lazarus to the utter amazement of everybody. My father insisted that I spend a year in healthful physical outdoor exercise to which I reluctantly consented. For most of this term I roamed in the mountains, loaded with a hunter's outfit and a bundle of books, and this contact with nature made me stronger in body as well as in mind. I thought and planned, and conceived many ideas almost as a rule delusive. The vision was clear enough but the knowledge of principles was very limited.

In one of my invention I proposed to convey letters and packages across the seas, through a submarine tube, in spherical containers of sufficient strength to resist the hydraulic pressure. The pumping plant, intended to force the water through the tube, was accurately figured and designed and all other particulars carefully worked out. Only one trifling detail, of no consequence, was lightly dismissed. I assumed an arbitrary velocity of the water and, what is more, took pleasure in making it high, thus arriving at a stupendous performance supported by faultless calculations. Subsequent reflections, however, on the resistance of pipes to fluid flow induced me to make this invention public property.

Another one of my projects was to construct a ring around the equator which would, of course, float freely and could be arrested in its spinning motion by reactionary forces, thus enabling travel at a rate of about one thousand miles an hour, impracticable by rail. The reader will smile. The plan was difficult of execution, I will admit, but not nearly so bad as that of a well known New York professor, who wanted to pump the air from the torrid to temperate zones, entirely forgetful of the fact that the Lord had provided a gigantic machine for this purpose.

Still another scheme, far more important and attractive, was to derive power from the rotational energy of terrestrial bodies. I had discovered that objects on the earth's surface owing to the diurnal rotation of the globe are carried by the same alternately in and against the direction of translatory movement. From this results a great change in momentum which could be utilized in the simplest imaginable manner to furnish motive effort in any habitable region of the world. I cannot find words to describe my disappointment when later I realized that I was in the predicament of Archimedes, who vainly sought for a fixed point in the universe. At the termination of my vacation, I was sent to the Poly-Technic School in Gratz, Styria (Austria), which my father had chosen as one of the oldest and best reputed institutions. That was the moment I had eagerly awaited and I began my studies under good auspices and firmly resolved to succeed. My previous training was above average, due to my father's teaching and opportunities afforded. I had acquired the knowledge of a number of languages and waded through the books of several libraries, picking up information more or less useful. Then again, for the first time, I could choose my subjects as I liked, and free-hand drawing was to bother me no more.

I had made up my mind to give my parents a surprise, and during the whole first year I regularly started my work at three o'clock in the morning and continued until eleven at night, no Sundays or holidays excepted. As most of my fellow-students took things easily, naturally I eclipsed all records. In the course of the year I passed through nine exams and the professors thought I deserved more than the highest qualifications. Armed with their flattering certificate, I went home for a short rest, expecting triumph, and was mortified when my father made light of these hard-won honors. That almost killed my ambition; but later, after he had died, I was pained to find a package of letters which the professors had written to him to the effect that unless he took me away from the Institution I would be killed through overwork. Thereafter I devoted myself chiefly to physics, mechanics and mathematical studies, spending the hours of leisure in the libraries. I had a veritable mania for finishing whatever I began, which often got me into difficulties. On one occasion I started to read the works of Voltaire, when I learned, to my dismay that there were close to one hundred large volumes in small print which that monster had written while drinking seventy-two cups of black coffee per diem. It had to be done, but when I laid aside that last book I was very glad, and said, "Never more!"

My first year's showing had won me the appreciation and friendship of several professors. Among these, Professor Rogner, who was teaching arithmetical subjects and geometry; Professor Poeschl, who held the chair of theoretical and experimental physics, and Dr. Alle, who taught integral calculus and specialized in differential equations. This scientist was the most brilliant lecturer to whom I ever listened. He took a special interest in my progress and would frequently remain for an hour or two in the lecture room, giving me problems to solve, in which I delighted. To him I explained a flying machine I had conceived, not an illusory invention, but one based on sound, scientific principles, which has become realizable through my turbine and will soon be given to the world. Both Professors Rogner and Poeschl were curious men. The former had peculiar ways of expressing himself and whenever he did so, there was a riot, followed by a long embarrassing pause. Professor Poeschl was a methodical and thoroughly grounded German. He had enormous feet, and hands like the paws of a bear, but all of his experiments were skillfully performed with clock-like precision and without a miss. It was in the second year of my studies that we received a Gramoe Dyname from Paris, having the horseshoe form of a laminated field magnet, and a wire wound armature with a commutator. It was connected up and various effects of the currents were shown. While Professor Poeschl was making demonstrations, running the machine was a motor, the brushes gave trouble, sparking badly, and I observed that it might be possible to operate a motor without these appliances. But he declared that it could not be done and did me the honor of delivering a lecture on the subject, at the conclusion he remarked, Mr. Tesla may accomplish great things, but he certainly will never do this. It would be equivalent to converting a steadily pulling force, like that of gravity into a rotary effort. It is a perpetual motion scheme, an impossible idea. But instinct is something which transcends knowledge. We have, undoubtedly, certain finer fibbers that enable us to perceive truths when logical deduction, or any other willful effort of the brain, is futile.

For a time I wavered, impressed by the professor's authority, but soon became convinced I was right and undertook the task with all the fire and boundless confidence of my youth. I started by first picturing in my mind a direct-current machine, running it and following the changing flow of the currents in the armature. Then I would imagine an alternator and investigate the progresses taking place in a similar manner. Next I would visualize systems comprising motors and generators and operate them in various ways. The images I saw were to me perfectly real and tangible. All my remaining term in Gratz was passed in intense but fruitless efforts of this kind, and I almost came to the conclusion that the problem was insolvable. In 1880 I went to Prague, Bohemia, carrying out my father's wish to complete my education at the University there. It was in that city that I made a decided advance, which consisted in detaching the commutator from the machine and studying the phenomena in this new aspect, but still without result. In the year following there was a sudden change in my views of life.

I realized that my parents had been making too great sacrifices on my account and resolved to relieve them of the burden. The wave of the American telephone had just reached the European continent and the system was to be installed in Budapest,

Hungary. It appeared an ideal opportunity, all the more as a friend of our family was at the head of the enterprise. It was here that I suffered the complete breakdown of the nerves to which I have referred. What I experienced during the period of the illness surpasses all belief. My sight and hearing were always extraordinary. I could clearly discern objects in the distance when others saw no trace of them. Several times in my boyhood I saved the houses of our neighbors from fire by hearing the faint crackling sounds which did not disturb their sleep, and calling for help. In 1899, when I was past forty and carrying on my experiments in Colorado, I could hear very distinctly thunderclaps at a distance of 550 miles. My ear was thus over thirteen times more sensitive, yet at that time I was, so to speak, stone deaf in comparison with the acuteness of my hearing while under the nervous strain.

In Budapest I could hear the ticking of a watch with three rooms between me and the timepiece. A fly alighting on a table in the room would cause a dull thud in my ear. A carriage passing at a distance of a few miles fairly shook my whole body. The whistle of a locomotive twenty or thirty miles away made the bench or chair on which I sat, vibrate so strongly that the pain was unbearable. The ground under my feet trembled continuously. I had to support my bed on rubber cushions to get any rest at all. The roaring noises from near and far often produced the effect of spoken words which would have frightened me had I not been able to resolve them into their accumulated components. The sun rays, when periodically intercepted, would cause blows of such force on my brain that they would stun me. I had to summon all my will power to pass under a bridge or other structure, as I experienced the crushing pressure on the skull. In the dark I had the sense of a bat, and could detect the presence of an object at a distance of twelve feet by a peculiar creepy sensation on the forehead. My pulse varied from a few to two hundred and sixty beats and all the tissues of my body with twitchings and tremors, which was perhaps hardest to bear. A renowned physician who have me daily large doses of Bromide of Potassium, pronounced my malady unique and incurable.

It is my eternal regret that I was not under the observation of experts in physiology and psychology at that time. I clung desperately to life, but never expected to recover. Can anyone believe that so hopeless a physical wreck could ever be transformed into a man of astonishing strength and tenacity; able to work thirty-eight years almost without a day's interruption, and find himself still strong and fresh in body and mind? Such is my case. A powerful desire to live and to continue the work and the assistance of a devoted friend, an athlete, accomplished the wonder. My health returned and with it the vigor of mind in attacking the problem again, I almost regretted that the struggle was soon to end. I had so much energy to spare. When I understood the task, it was not with a resolve such as men often make. With me it was a sacred vow, a question of life and death. I knew that I would perish if I failed. Now I felt that the battle was won. Back in the deep recesses of the brain was the solution, but I could net yet give it outward expression.

One afternoon, which is ever present in my recollection, I was enjoying a walk with my friend in the City Park and reciting poetry. At that age, I knew entire books by heart, word for word. One of these was Goethe's "Faust." The sun was just setting and reminded me of the glorious passage, "Sie ruckt und weight, der Tag ist uberlebt, Dort eilt sie hin und fordert neues Leben. Oh, da kein Flugel mich vom Boden hebt Ihr nach und immer nach zu streben! Ein schsner Traum indessen sie entweicht, Ach, au des Geistes Flygein wird so leicht Kein korperlicher Flugel sich gesellen!" As I uttered these inspiring words the idea came like a flash of lightening and in an instant the truth was revealed. I drew with a stick on the sand, the diagram shown six years later in my address before the American Institute of Electrical Engineers, and my companion understood them perfectly. The images I saw were wonderfully sharp and clear and had the solidity of metal and stone, so much so that I told him, "See my motor here; watch me reverse it." I cannot begin to describe my emotions. Pygmalion seeing his statue come to life could not have been more deeply moved. A thousand secrets of nature which I might have stumbled upon accidentally, I would have given for that one which I had wrested from her against all odds and at the peril of my existence...

Chapter 4—Tesla Coil and Transformer

FOR a while I gave myself up entirely to the intense enjoyment of picturing machines and devising new forms. It was a mental state of happiness about as complete as I have ever known in life. Ideas came in an uninterrupted stream and the only difficulty I had was to hold them fast. The pieces of apparatus I conceived were to me absolutely real and tangible in every detail even to the minutest marks and signs of wear. I delighted in imagining the motors constantly running, for in this way they presented to the mind's eye a fascinating sight. When natural inclination develops into a passionate desire, one advances towards his goal in seven-league boots. In less than two months I evolved virtually all the types of motors and modifications of the system which are now identified with my name, and which are used under many other names all over the world. It was, perhaps, providential that the necessities of existence commanded a temporary halt to this consuming activity of the mind.

I came to Budapest prompted by a premature report concerning the telephone enterprise and, as irony of fate willed it, I had to accept a position as draughts man in the Central Telegraph Office of the Hungarian Government at a salary which I deem it my privilege not to disclose. Fortunately, I soon won the interest of the Inspector-in-Chief and was thereafter employed on calculations, designs and estimates in connection with new installations, until the Telephone exchange started, when I took charge of the same. The knowledge and practical experience I gained in the course of this work, was most valuable and the employment gave me ample opportunities for the exercise of my inventive faculties. I made several improvements in the Central Station apparatus and perfected a telephone repeater or amplifier which was never patented or publicly described but would be creditable to me even today. In recognition of my efficient assistance the organizer of the undertaking, Mr. Puskas, upon disposing of his business in Budapest, offered me a position in Paris which I gladly accepted.

I never can forget the deep impression that magic city produced on my mind. For several days after my arrival, I roamed through the streets in utter bewilderment of the new spectacle. The attractions were many and irresistible, but, alas, the income was spent as soon as received. When Mr. Puskas asked me how I was getting along in the new sphere, I described the situation accurately in the statement that "The last twenty-nine days of the month are the toughest." I led a rather strenuous life in what would now be termed "Rooseveltian fashion." Every morning, regardless of the weather, I would go from the Boulevard St. Marcel, where I resided, to a bathing house on the Seine; plunge into the water, loop the circuit twenty-seven times and then walk an hour to reach Ivry, where the Company's factory was located. There I would have a wood-chopper's breakfast at half-past seven o'clock and then eagerly await the lunch hour, in the meanwhile cracking hard nuts for the Manager of the Works, Mr. Charles Bachelor, who was an intimate friend and assistant of Edison. Here I was thrown in contact with a few Americans who fairly fell in love with my because of my proficiency in Billiards! To these men I explained my invention and one of them, Mr. D. Cunningham, foreman of the Mechanical Department, offered to form a stock company. The proposal seemed to me comical in the extreme. I did not have the faintest conception of what he meant, except that it was an American way of doing things. Nothing came of it, however, and during the next few months I had to travel from one place to another in France and Germany to cure the ills of the power plants.

On my return to Paris, I submitted to one of the administrators of the Company, Mr. Rau, a plan for improving their dynamos and was given an opportunity. My success was complete and the delighted directors accorded me the privilege of developing automatic regulators which were much desired. Shortly after, there was some trouble with the lighting plant which had been installed at the new railroad station in Strasbourg, Alsace. The wiring was defective and on the occasion of the opening ceremonies, a large part of a wall was blown out through a short-circuit, right in the presence of old Emperor William I. The German Government refused to take the plant and the French Company was facing a serious loss. On account of my knowledge of the German language and past experience, I was entrusted with the difficult task of straightening out matters and early in 1883, I went to Strasbourg on that mission.

Some of the incidents in that city have left an indelible record on my memory. By a curious coincidence, a number of the men who subsequently achieve fame, lived there about that time. In later life I used to say, "There were bacteria of greatness in that old town." Others caught the disease, but I escaped!" The practical work, correspondence, and conferences with officials kept me preoccupied day and night, but as soon as I was able to manage, I undertook the construction of a simple motor in a mechanical shop opposite the railroad station, having brought with me from Paris some material for that purpose. The consummation of the experiment was, however, delayed until the summer of that year, when I finally had the satisfaction of seeing the rotation effected by alternating currents of different phase, and without sliding contacts or commutator, as I had conceived a year before. It was an exquisite pleasure but not to compare with the delirium of joy following the first revelation. Among my new friends was the former Mayor of the city, Mr. Sauzin, whom I had already, in a measure, acquainted with this and other inventions of mine and whose support I endeavoured to enlist. He was sincerely devoted to me and put my project before several wealthy persons, but to my mortification, found no response. He wanted to help me in every possible way and the approach of the first of July, 1917, happens to remind me of a form of "assistance" I received from that charming man, which was not financial, but none the less appreciated. In 1870, when the Germans invaded the country, Mr. Sauzin had buried a good sized allotment of St. Estephe of 1801 and he came to the conclusion that he knew no worthier person than myself, to consume that precious beverage. This, I may say, is one of the unforgettable incidents to which I have referred. My friend urged me to return to Paris as soon as possible and seek support there. This I was anxious to do, but my work and negotiations were protracted, owing to all sorts of petty obstacles I encountered, so that at times the situation seemed hopeless. Just to give an idea of German thoroughness and "efficiency," I may mention here a rather funny experience.

An incandescent lamp of 16 c.p. was to be placed in a hallway, and upon selected the proper location, I ordered the "monteur" to run the wires. After working for a while, he concluded that the engineer had to be consulted and this was done. The latter made several objections but ultimately agreed that the lamp should be placed two inches from the spot I had assigned, whereupon the work proceeded. Then the engineer became worried and told me that Inspector Averdeck should be notified. That important person was called, he investigated, debated, and decided that the lamp should be shifted back two inches, which was the placed I had marked! It was not long, however, before Averdeck got cold feet himself and advised me that he had informed Ober-Inspector Hieronimus of the matter and that I should await his decision. It was several days before the Ober-Inspector was able to free himself of other pressing duties, but at last he arrived and a two hour debate followed, when he decided to move the lamp two inches further. My hopes that this was the final act, were shattered when the Ober-Inspector returned and said to me, "Regierungsrath

Funke is particular that I would not dare to give an order for placing this lamp without his explicit approval." Accordingly, arrangements for a visit from that great man were made. We started cleaning up and polishing early in the morning, and when Funke came with his retinue he was ceremoniously received. After two hours of deliberation, he suddenly exclaimed, "I must be going!," and pointing to a place on the ceiling, he ordered me to put the lamp there. It was the exact spot which I had originally chosen! So it went day after day with variations, but I was determined to achieve, at whatever cost, and in the end my efforts were rewarded.

By the spring of 1884, all the differences were adjusted, the plant formally accepted, and I returned to Paris with pleasing anticipation. One of the administrators had promised me a liberal compensation in case I succeeded, as well as a fair consideration of the improvements I had made to their dynamos and I hoped to realize a substantial sum. There were three administrators, whom I shall designate as A, B, and C for convenience. When I called on A, he told me that B had the say. This gentleman thought that only C could decide, and the latter was quite sure that A alone had the power to act. After several laps of this circulus viciousus, it dawned upon me that my reward was a castle in Spain. The utter failure of my attempts to raise capital for development was another disappointment, and when Mr. Bachelor pressed me to go to America with a view of redesigning the Edison machines, I determined to try my fortunes in the Land of Golden Promise. But the chance was nearly missed. I liquefied my modest assets, secured accommodations and found myself at the railroad station as the train was pulling out. At that moment, I discovered that my money and tickets were gone. What to do was the question. Hercules had plenty of time to deliberate, but I had to decide while running alongside the train with opposite feeling surging in my brain like condenser oscillations. Resolve, helped by dexterity, won out in the nick of time and upon passing through the usual experience, as trivial and unpleasant, I managed to embark for New York with the remnants of my belongings, some poems and articles I had written, and a package of calculations relating to solutions of an unsolvable integral and my flying machine. During the voyage I sat most of the time at the stern of the ship watching for an opportunity to save somebody from a watery grave, without the slightest thought of danger. Later, when I had absorbed some of the practical American sense, I shivered at the recollection and marveled at my former folly. The meeting with Edison was a memorable event in my life. I was amazed at this wonderful man who, without early advantages and scientific training, had accomplished so much. I had studied a dozen languages, delved in literature and art, and had spent my best years in libraries reading all sorts of stuff that fell into my hands, from Newton's "Principia" to the novels of Paul de Kock, and felt that most of my life had been squandered. But it did not take long before I recognized that it was the best thing I could have done. Within a few weeks I had won Edison's confidence, and it came about in this way.

The S.S. Oregon, the fastest passenger steamer at that time, had both of its lighting machines disabled and its sailing was delayed. As the superstructure had been built after their installation, it was impossible to remove them from the hold. The predicament was a serious one and Edison was much annoyed. In the evening I took the necessary instruments with me and went aboard the vessel where I stayed for the night. The dynamos were in bad condition, having several short-circuits and breaks, but with the assistance of the crew, I succeeded in putting them in good shape. At five o'clock in the morning, when passing along Fifth Avenue on my way to the shop, I met Edison with Bachelor and a few others, as they were returning home to retire. "Here is our Parisian running around at night," he said. When I told him that I was coming from the Oregon and had repaired both machines, he looked at me in silence and walked away without another word. But when he had gone some distance I heard him remark, "Bachelor, this is a good man." And from that time on I had full freedom in directing the work. For nearly a year my regular hours were from 10:30 A.M. until 5 o'clock the next morning without a day's exception. Edison said to me, "I have had many hard working assistants, but you take the cake." During this period I designed twenty-four different types of standard machines with short cores and uniform pattern, which replaced the old ones. The Manager had promised me fifty thousand dollars on the completion of this task, but it turned out to be a practical joke. This gave me a painful shock and I resigned my position.

Immediately thereafter, some people approached me with the proposal of forming an arc light company under my name, to which I agreed. Here finally, was an opportunity to develop the motor, but when I broached the subject to my new associates they said, "No, we want the arc lamp. We don't care for this alternating current of yours." In 1886 my system of arc lighting was perfected and adopted for factory and municipal lighting, and I was free, but with no other possession than a beautifully engraved certificate of stock of hypothetical value. Then followed a period of struggle in the new medium for which I was not fitted, but the reward came in the end, and in April, 1887, the TESLA Electric Co. was organized, providing a laboratory and facilities. The motors I built there were exactly as I had imagined them. I made no attempt to improve the design, but merely reproduced the pictures as they appeared to my vision and the operation was always as I expected.

In the early part of 1888, an arrangement was made with the Westinghouse Company for the manufacture of the motors on a large scale. But great difficulties had still to be overcome. My system was based on the use of low frequency currents and the Westinghouse experts had adopted 133 cycles with the objects of securing advantages in transformation. They did not want to depart with their standard forms of apparatus and my efforts had to be concentrated upon adapting the motor to these conditions. Another necessity was to produce a motor capable of running efficiently at this frequency on two wire, which was not an easy accomplishment. At the close of 1889, however, my services in Pittsburgh being no longer essential, I returned to New York and resumed experimental work in a Laboratory on Grand Street, where I began immediately the design of high-frequency machines. The problems of construction in this unexplored field were novel and quite peculiar, and I encountered many difficulties. I rejected the inductor type, fearing that it might not yield perfect sine waves, which were so important to resonant action. Had it not been for this, I could have saved myself a great deal of labour. Another discouraging feature of the high-frequency alternator seemed to be the inconstancy of speed which threatened to impose serious limitations to its use. I had already noted in my demonstrations before the American Institution of Electrical Engineers, that several times the tune was lost, necessitating readjustment, and did not yet foresee what I discovered long afterwards, a means of operating a machine of this kind at a speed constant to such a degree as not to vary more than a small fraction of one revolution between the extremes of load. From many other considerations, it appeared desirable to invent a simpler device for the production of electric oscillations.

In 1856, Lord Kelvin had exposed the theory of the condenser discharge, but no practical application of that important knowledge was made. I saw the possibilities and undertook the development of induction apparatus on this principle. My progress was so rapid as to enable me to exhibit at my lecture in 1891, a coil giving sparks of five inches. On that occasion I frankly told the engineers of a defect involved in the transformation by the new method, namely, the loss in the spark gap. Subsequent investigation showed that no matter what medium is employed, be it air, hydrogen, mercury vapour, oil, or a stream of electrons, the efficiency is the same. It is a law very much like the governing of the conversion of mechanical energy. We may drop a weight from a certain height vertically down, or carry it to the lower level along any devious path; it is immaterial insofar as the amount of work is concerned. Fortunately however, this drawback is not fatal, as by proper proportioning of the resonant, circuits of an efficiency of 85 percent is attainable. Since my early announcement of the invention, it has come into universal use and wrought a revolution in many departments, but a still greater future awaits it. When in 1900 I obtained powerful discharges of 1,000 feet and flashed a current around the globe, I was reminded of the first tiny spark I observed in my Grand Street laboratory and was thrilled by sensations akin to those I felt when I discovered the rotating magnetic field.

Chapter 5—The Influences That Shape Our Destiny

AS I review the events of my past life I realize how subtle are the influences that shape our destinies. An incident of my youth may serve to illustrate. One winter's day I managed to climb a steep mountain, in company with other boys. The snow was quite deep and a warm southerly wind made it just suitable for our purpose. We amused ourselves by throwing balls which would roll down a certain distance, gathering more or less snow, and we tried to outdo one another in this sport. Suddenly a ball was seen to go beyond the limit, swelling to enormous proportions until it became as big as a house and plunged thundering into the valley below with a force that made the ground tremble. I looked on spellbound incapable of understanding what had happened. For weeks afterward the picture of the avalanche was before my eyes and I wondered how anything so small could grow to such an immense size.

Ever since that time the magnification of feeble actions fascinated me, and when, years later, I took up the experimental study of mechanical and electrical resonance, I was keenly interested from the very start. Possibly, had it not been for that early powerful impression I might not have followed up the little spark I obtained with my coil and never developed my best invention, the true history of which I will tell. Many technical men, very able in their special departments, but dominated by a pedantic spirit and nearsighted, have asserted that excepting the induction motor, I have given the world little of practical use. This is a grievous mistake. A new idea must not be judged by its immediate results. My alternating system of power transmission came at a psychological moment, as a long sought answer to pressing industrial questions, and although considerable resistance had to be overcome and opposing interests reconciled, as usual, the commercial introduction could not be long delayed. Now, compare this situation with that confronting my turbines, for example. One should think that so simple and beautiful an invention, possessing many features of an ideal motor, should be adopted at once and, undoubtedly, it would under similar conditions. But the prospective effect of the rotating field was not to render worthless existing machinery; on the contrary, it was to give it additional value. The system lent itself to new enterprise as well as to improvement of the old. My turbine is an advance of a character entirely different. It is a radical departure in the sense that its success would mean the abandonment of the antiquated types of prime movers on which

78

billions of dollars have been spent. Under such circumstances, the progress must needs be slow and perhaps the greatest impediment is encountered in the prejudicial opinions created in the minds of experts by organized opposition.

Only the other day, I had a disheartening experience when I met my friend and former assistant, Charles F. Scott, now professor of Electric Engineering at Yale. I had not seen him for a long time and was glad to have an opportunity for a little chat at my office. Our conversation, naturally enough, drifted on my turbine and I became heated to a high degree. "Scott," I exclaimed, carried away by the vision of a glorious future, "My turbine will scrap all the heat engines in the world." Scott stroked his chin and looked away thoughtfully, as though making a mental calculation. "That will make quite a pile of scrap," he said, and left without another word.

These and other inventions of mine, however, were nothing more than steps forward in a certain directions. In evolving them, I simply followed the inborn instinct to improve the present devices without any special thought of our far more imperative necessities. The "Magnifying Transmitter" was the product of labours extending through years, having for their chief object, the solution of problems which are infinitely more important to mankind than mere industrial development.

If my memory serves me right, it was in November, 1890, that I performed a laboratory experiment which was one of the most extraordinary and spectacular ever recorded in the annals of Science. In investigating the behavior of high frequency currents, I had satisfied myself that an electric field of sufficient intensity could be produced in a room to light up electrode less vacuum tubes. Accordingly, a transformer was built to test the theory and the first trial proved a marvelous success. It is difficult to appreciate what those strange phenomena meant at the time. We crave for new sensations, but soon become indifferent to them. The wonders of yesterday are today common occurrences. When my tubes were first publicly exhibited, they were viewed with amazement impossible to describe. From all parts of the world, I received urgent invitations and numerous honors and other flattering inducements were offered to me, which I declined. But in 1892 the demand became irresistible and I went to London where I delivered a lecture before the institution of Electrical Engineers.

It has been my intention to leave immediately for Paris in compliance with a similar obligation, but Sir James Dewar insisted on my appearing before the Royal Institution. I was a man of firm resolve, but succumbed easily to the forceful arguments of the great Scotsman. He pushed me into a chair and poured out half a glass of a wonderful brown fluid which sparkled in all sorts of iridescent colors and tasted like nectar. "Now," said he, "you are sitting in Faraday's chair and you are enjoying whiskey he used to drink." (Which did not interest me very much, as I had altered my opinion concerning strong drink). The next evening I have a demonstration before the Royal Institution, at the termination of which, Lord Rayleigh addressed the audience and his generous words gave me the first start in these endeavors. I fled from London and later from Paris, to escape favors showered upon me, and journeyed to my home, where I passed through a most painful ordeal and illness. Upon regaining my health, I began to formulate plans for the resumption of work in America. Up to that time I never realized that I possessed any particular gift of discovery, but Lord Rayleigh, whom I always considered as an ideal man of science, had said so and if that was the case, I felt that I should concentrate on some big idea. At this time, as at many other times in the past, my thoughts turned towards my Mother's teaching. The gift of mental power comes from God, Divine Being, and if we concentrate our minds on that truth, we become in tune with this great power. My Mother had taught me to seek all truth in the Bible; therefore I devoted the next few months to the study of this work.

One day, as I was roaming the mountains, I sought shelter from an approaching storm. The sky became overhung with heavy clouds, but somehow the rain was delayed until, all of a sudden, there was a lightening flash and a few moments after, a deluge. This observation set me thinking. It was manifest that the two phenomena were closely related, as cause and effect, and a little reflection led me to the conclusion that the electrical energy involved in the precipitation of the water was inconsiderable, the function of the lightening being much like that of a sensitive trigger. Here was a stupendous possibility of achievement. If we could produce electric effects of the required quality, this whole planet and the conditions of existence on it could be transformed. The sun raises the water of the oceans and winds drive it to distant regions where it remains in a state of most delicate balance. If it were in our power to upset it when and wherever desired, this might life sustaining stream could be at will controlled. We could irrigate arid deserts, create lakes and rivers, and provide motive power in unlimited amounts. This would be the most efficient way of harnessing the sun to the uses of man. The consummation depended on our ability to develop electric forces of the order of those in nature.

It seemed a hopeless undertaking, but I made up my mind to try it and immediately on my return to the United States in the summer of 1892, after a short visit to my friends in Watford, England; work was begun which was to me all the more attractive, because a means of the same kind was necessary for the successful transmission of energy without wires. At this time I made a further careful study of the Bible, and discovered the key in Revelation. The first gratifying result was obtained in the spring of the succeeding year, when I reaching a tension of about 100,000,000 volts—one hundred million volts -- with my conical coil, which I figured was the voltage of a flash of lightening. Steady progress was made until the destruction of my laboratory by fire, in 1895, as may be judged from an article by T.C. Martin which appeared in the April number of the Century Magazine. This calamity set me back in many ways and most of that year had to be devoted to planning and reconstruction. However, as soon as circumstances permitted, I returned to the task.

Although I knew that higher electric-motive forces were attainable with apparatus of larger dimensions, I had an instinctive perception that the object could be accomplished by the proper design of a comparatively small and compact transformer. In carrying on tests with a secondary in the form of flat spiral, as illustrated in my patents, the absence of streamers surprised me, and it was not long before I discovered that this was due to the position of the turns and their mutual action. Profiting from this observation, I resorted to the use of a high tension conductor with turns of considerable diameter, sufficiently separated to keep down the distributed capacity, while at the same time preventing undue accumulation of the charge at any point. The application of this principle enabled me to produce pressures of over 100,000,000 volts, which was about the limit obtainable without risk of accident. A photograph of my transmitter built in my laboratory at Houston Street, was published in the Electrical Review of November, 1898.

In order to advance further along this line, I had to go into the open, and in the spring of 1899, having completed preparations for the erection of a wireless plant, I went to Colorado where I remained for more than one year. Here I introduced other improvements and refinements which made it possible to generate currents of any tension that may be desired. Those who are interested will find some information in regard to the experiments I conducted there in my article, "The Problem of Increasing Human Energy," in the Century Magazine of June 1900, to which I have referred on a previous occasion.

I will be quite explicit on the subject of my magnifying transformer so that it will be clearly understood. In the first place, it is a resonant transformer, with a secondary in which the parts, charged to a high potential, are of considerable area and arranged in space along ideal enveloping surfaces of very large radii of curvature, and at proper distances from one another, thereby insuring a small electric surface density everywhere, so that no leak can occur even if the conductor is bare. It is suitable for any frequency, from a few to many thousands of cycles per second, and can be used in the production of currents of tremendous volume and moderate pressure, or of smaller amperage and immense electromotive force. The maximum electric tension is merely dependent on the curvature of the surfaces on which the charged elements are situated and the area of the latter. Judging from my past experience there is no limit to the possible voltage developed; any amount is practicable. On the other hand, currents of many thousands of amperes may be obtained in the antenna. A plant of but very moderate dimensions is required for such performances. Theoretically, a terminal of less than 90 feet in diameter is sufficient to develop an electromotive force of that magnitude, while for antenna currents of from 2,000-4,000 amperes at the usual frequencies, it need not be larger than 30 feet in diameter. In a more restricted meaning, this wireless transmitter is one in which the Hertzwave radiation is an entirely negligible quantity as compared with the whole energy, under which condition the damping factor is extremely small and an enormous charge is stored in the elevated capacity. Such a circuit may then be excited with impulses of any kind, even of low frequency and it will yield sinusoidal and continuous oscillations like those of an alternator. Taken in the narrowest significance of the term, however, it is a resonant transformer which, besides possessing these qualities, is accurately proportioned to fit the globe and its electrical constants and properties, by virtue of which design it becomes highly efficient and effective in the wireless transmission of energy. Distance is then absolutely eliminated, there being no diminuation in the intensity of the transmitted impulses. It is even possible to make the actions increase with the distance from the plane, according to an exact mathematical law. This invention was one of a number comprised in my "World System" of wireless transmission which I undertook to commercialize on my return to New York in 1900.

As to the immediate purposes of my enterprise, they were clearly outlined in a technical statement of that period from which I quote, "The world system has resulted from a combination of several original discoveries made by the inventor in the course of long continued research and experimentation. It makes possible not only the instantaneous and precise wireless transmission of any kind of signals, messages or characters, to all parts of the world, but also the inter-connection of the existing telegraph, telephone, and other signal stations without any change in their present equipment. By its means, for instance, a telephone subscriber here may call up and talk to any other subscriber on the Earth. An inexpensive receiver, not bigger than a watch, will enable him to listen anywhere, on land or sea, to a speech delivered or music played in some other place, however distant."

These examples are cited merely to give an idea of the possibilities of this great scientific advance, which annihilates distance and makes that perfect natural conductor, the Earth, available for all the innumerable purposes which human ingenuity has found for a line-wire. One far-reaching result of this is that any device capable of being operated through one or more wires (at a distance obviously restricted) can likewise be actuated, without artificial conductors and with the same facility and accuracy, at distances to which there are no limits other than those imposed by the physical dimensions of the earth. Thus, not only will entirely new fields for commercial exploitation be opened up by this ideal method of transmission, but the old ones vastly extended. The World System is based on the application of the following import and inventions and discoveries:

1.) The Tesla Transformer: This apparatus is in the production of electrical vibrations as revolutionary as gunpowder was in warfare. Currents many times stronger than any ever generated in the usual ways and sparks over one hundred feet long, have been produced by the inventor with an instrument of this kind.

2.) The Magnifying Transmitter: This is Tesla's best invention, a peculiar transformer specially adapted to excite the earth, which is in the transmission of electrical energy when the telescope is in astronomical observation. By the use of this marvelous device, he has already set up electrical movements of greater intensity than those of lightening and passed a current, sufficient to light more than two hundred incandescent lamps, around the Earth.

3.) The Tesla Wireless System: This system comprises a number of improvements and is the only means known for transmitting economically electrical energy to a distance without wires. Careful tests and measurements in connection with an experimental station of great activity, erected by the inventor in Colorado, have demonstrated that power in any desired amount can be conveyed, clear across the Globe if necessary, with a loss not exceeding a few per cent.

4.) The Art of Individualization: This invention of Tesla is to primitive Tuning, what refined language is to unarticulated expression. It makes possible the transmission of signals or messages absolutely secret and exclusive both in the active and passive aspect, that is, non-interfering as well as non-interferable. Each signal is like an individual of unmistakable identity and there is virtually no limit to the number of stations or instruments which can be simultaneously operated without the slightest mutual disturbance.

5.) The Terrestrial Stationary Waves: This wonderful discovery, popularly explained, means that the Earth is responsive to electrical vibrations of definite pitch, just as a tuning fork to certain waves of sound. These particular electrical vibrations, capable of powerfully exciting the Globe, lend themselves to innumerable uses of great importance commercially and in many other respects. The "first World System" power plant can be put in operation in nine months. With this power plant, it will be practicable to attain electrical activities up to ten million horsepower and it is designed to serve for as many technical achievements as are possible without due expense.

Among these are the following:

1.   The interconnection of existing telegraph exchanges or offices all over the world;

2.   The establishment of a secret and non-interferable government telegraph service;

3.   The interconnection of all present telephone exchanges or offices around the Globe;

4.   The universal distribution of general news by telegraph or telephone, in conjunction with the Press;

5. The establishment of such a "World System" of intelligence transmission for exclusive private use;

6. The interconnection and operation of all stock tickers of the world;

7. The establishment of a World system—of musical distribution, etc.;

8. The universal registration of time by cheap clocks indicating the hour with astronomical precision and requiring no attention whatever;

9. The world transmission of typed or handwritten characters, letters, checks, etc.;

10. The establishment of a universal marine service enabling the navigators of all ships to steer perfectly without compass, to determine the exact location, hour and speak; to prevent collisions and disasters, etc.;

11. The inauguration of a system of world printing on land and sea;

12. The world reproduction of photographic pictures and all kinds of drawings or records..."

I also proposed to make demonstration in the wireless transmission of power on a small scale, but sufficient to carry conviction. Besides these, I referred to other and incomparably more important applications of my discoveries which will be disclosed at some future date. A plant was built on Long Island with a tower 187 feet high, having a spherical terminal about 68 feet in diameter. These dimensions were adequate for the transmission of virtually any amount of energy. Originally, only from 200 to 300 K.W. were provided, but I intended to employ later several thousand horsepower. The transmitter was to emit a wave-complex of special characteristics and I had devised a unique method of telephonic control of any amount of energy. The tower was destroyed two years ago (1917) but my projects are being developed and another one, improved in some features will be constructed.

On this occasion I would contradict the widely circulated report that the structure was demolished by the Government, which owing to war conditions, might have created prejudice in the minds of those who may not know that the papers, which thirty years ago conferred upon me the honor of American citizenship, are always kept in a safe, while my orders, diplomas, degrees, gold medals and other distinctions are packed away in old trunks. If this report had a foundation, I would have been refunded a large sum of money which I expended in the construction of the tower. On the contrary, it was in the interest of the Government to preserver it, particularly as it would have made possible, to mention just one valuable result, the location of a submarine in any part of the world. My plant, services, and all my improvements have always been at the disposal of the officials and ever since the outbreak of the European conflict, I have been working at a sacrifice on several inventions of mine relating to aerial navigation, ship propulsion and wireless transmission, which are of the greatest importance to the country. Those who are well informed know that my ideas have revolutionized the industries of the United States and I am not aware that there lives an inventor who has been, in this respect, as fortunate as myself,—especially as regards the use of his improvements in the war.

I have refrained from publicly expressing myself on this subject before, as it seemed improper to dwell on personal matters while all the world was in dire trouble. I would add further, in view of various rumors which have reached me, that Mr. J. Pierpont Morgan did not interest himself with me in a business way, but in the same large spirit in which he has assisted many other pioneers. He carried out his generous promise to the letter and it would have been most unreasonable to expect from him anything more. He had the highest regard for my attainments and gave me every evidence of his complete faith in my ability to ultimately achieve what I had set out to do. I am unwilling to accord to some small-minded and jealous individuals the satisfaction of having thwarted my efforts. These men are to me nothing more than microbes of a nasty disease. My project was retarded by laws of nature. The world was not prepared for it. It was too far ahead of time, but the same laws will prevail in the end and make it a triumphal success.

Chapter 6—The Magnifying Transmitter

NO subject to which I have ever devoted myself has called for such concentration of mind, and strained to so dangerous a degree the finest fibbers of my brain, as the systems of which the Magnifying transmitter is the foundation. I put all the intensity and vigor of youth in the development of the rotating field discoveries, but those early labours were of a different character. Although strenuous in the extreme, they did not involve that keen and exhausting discernment which had to be exercised in attacking the many problems of the wireless.

Despite my rare physical endurance at that period, the abused nerves finally rebelled and I suffered a complete collapse, just as the consummation of the long and difficult task was almost in sight. Without doubt I would have paid a greater penalty later, and very likely my career would have been prematurely terminated, had not providence equipped me with a safety device, which seemed to improve with advancing years and unfailingly comes to play when my forces are at an end. So long as it operates I am safe from danger, due to overwork, which threatens other inventors, and incidentally, I need no vacations which are indispensable to most people. When I am all but used up, I simply do as the darkies who "naturally fall asleep while white folks worry."

To venture a theory out of my sphere, the body probably accumulates little by little a definite quantity of some toxic agent and I sink into a nearly lethargic state which lasts half an hour to the minute. Upon awakening I have the sensation as though the events immediately preceding had occurred very long ago, and if I attempt to continue the interrupted train of thought I feel veritable nausea. Involuntarily, I then turn to other and am surprised at the freshness of the mind and ease with which I overcome obstacles that had baffled me before. After weeks or months, my passion for the temporarily abandoned invention returns and I invariably find answers to all the vexing questions, with scarcely any effort. In this connection, I will tell of an extraordinary experience which may be of interest to students of psychology. I had produced a striking phenomenon with my grounded transmitter and was endeavoring to ascertain its true significance in relation to the currents propagated through the earth. It seemed a hopeless undertaking, and for more than a year I worked unremittingly, but in vain. This profound study so entirely absorbed me, that I became forgetful of everything else, even of my undermined health. At last, as I was at the point of breaking down, nature applied the preservative inducing lethal sleep. Regaining my senses, I realized with consternation that I was unable to visualize scenes from my life except those of infancy, the very first ones that had entered my consciousness. Curiously enough, these appeared before my vision with startling distinctness and afforded me welcome relief. Night after night, when retiring, I would think of them and more and more of my previous existence was revealed. The image of my mother was always the principal figure in the spectacle that slowly unfolded, and a consuming desire to see her again gradually took possession of me. This feeling grew so strong that I resolved to drop all work and satisfy my longing, but I found it too hard to break away from the laboratory, and several months elapsed during which I had succeeded in reviving all the impressions of my past life, up to the spring of 1892. In the next picture that came out of the mist of oblivion, I saw myself at the Hotel de la Paix in Paris, just coming to from one of my peculiar sleeping spells, which had been caused by prolonged exertion of the brain. Imagine the pain and distress I felt, when it flashed upon my mind that a dispatch was handed to me at that very moment, bearing the sad news that my mother was dying. I remembered how I made the long journey home without an hour of rest and how she passed away after weeks of agony. It was especially remarkable that during all this period of partially obliterated memory, I was fully alive to everything touching on the subject of my research. I could recall the smallest detail and the least insignificant observations in my experiments and even recite pages of text and complex mathematical formulae.

My belief is firm in a law of compensation. The true rewards are ever in proportion to the labour and sacrifices made. This is one of the reasons why I feel certain that of all my inventions, the magnifying Transmitter will prove most important and valuable to future generations. I am prompted to this prediction, not so much by thoughts of the commercial and industrial revolution which it will surely bring about, but of the humanization consequences of the many achievements it makes possible. Considerations of mere utility weigh little in the balance against the higher benefits of civilization. We are confronted with portentous problems which can not be solved just by providing for our material existence, however abundantly. On the contrary, progress in this direction is fraught with hazards and perils not less menacing than those born from want and suffering. If we were to release the energy of atoms or discover some other way of developing cheap and unlimited power at any point on the globe, this accomplishment, instead of being a blessing, might bring disaster to mankind in giving rise to dissension and anarchy, which would ultimately result in the enthronement of the hated regime of force. The greatest good will come from technical improvements tending to unification and harmony, and my wireless transmitter is preeminently such. By its means, the human voice and likeness will be reproduced everywhere and factories driven thousands of miles from waterfalls furnishing power. Aerial machines will be propelled around the earth without a stop and the sun's energy controlled to create lakes and rivers for motive purposes and transformation of arid deserts into fertile land. Its introduction for telegraphic, telephonic and similar uses, will automatically cut out the static and all other interferences which at present, impose narrow limits to the application of the wireless. This is a timely topic on which a few words might not be amiss.

During the past decade a number of people have arrogantly claimed that they had succeeded in doing away with this impediment. I have carefully examined all of the arrangements described and tested most of them long before they were publicly disclosed, but the finding was uniformly negative. Recent official statement from the U.S. Navy may, perhaps, have taught some beguilable news editors how to appraise these announcements at their real worth. As a rule, the attempts are based on theories so fallacious, that whenever they come to my notice, I can not help thinking in a light vein. Quite recently a new discovery was heralded, with a deafening flourish of trumpets, but it proved another case of a mountain bringing forth a mouse. This reminds me of an exciting incident which took place a year ago, when I was conducting my experiments with currents of high frequency.

Steve Brodie had just jumped off the Brooklyn Bridge. The feat has been vulgarized since by imitators, but the first report electrified New York. I was very impressionable then and frequently spoke of the daring printer. On a hot afternoon I felt the necessity of refreshing myself and stepped into one of the popular thirty thousand institutions of this great city, where a delicious twelve per cent beverage was served, which can now be had only by making a trip to the poor and devastated countries of Europe. The attendance was large and not over-distinguished and a matter was discussed which gave me an admirable opening for the careless remark, "This is what I said when I jumped off the bridge." No sooner had I uttered these words, than I felt like the companion of Timothens, in the poem of Schiller. In an instant there was pandemonium and a dozen voices cried, "It is Brodie!" I threw a quarter on the counter and bolted for the door, but the crowd was at my heels with yells, "Stop, Steve!", which must have been misunderstood, for many persons tried to hold me up as I ran frantically for my haven of refuge. By darting around corners I fortunately managed, through the medium of a fire escape, to reach the laboratory, where I threw off my coat, camouflaged myself as a hardworking blacksmith and started the forge. But these precautions proved unnecessary, as I had eluded my pursuers. For many years afterward, at night, when imagination turns into specters the trifling troubles of the day, I often thought, as I tossed on the bed, what my fate would have been, had the mob caught me and found out that I was not Steve Brodie!

Now the engineer who lately gave an account before a technical body of a novel remedy against static based on a "heretofore unknown law of nature," seems to have been as reckless as myself when he contended that these disturbances propagate up and down, while those of a transmitter proceed along the earth. It would mean that a condenser as this globe, with its gaseous envelope, could be charged and discharged in a manner quite contrary to the fundamental teachings propounded in every elemental textbook of physics. Such a supposition would have been condemned as erroneous, even in Franklin's time, for the facts bearing on this were then well known and the identity between atmospheric electricity and that developed by machines was fully established. Obviously, natural and artificial disturbances propagate through the earth and the air in exactly the same way, and both set up electromotive forces in the horizontal, as well as vertical sense. Interference can not be overcome by any such methods as were proposed. The truth is this: In the air the potential increases at the rate of about fifty volts per foot of elevation, owing to which there may be a difference of pressure amounting to twenty, or even forty thousand volts between the upper and lower ends of the antenna. The masses of the charged atmosphere are constantly in motion and give up electricity to the conductor, not continuously, but rather disruptively, this producing a grinding noise in a sensitive telephonic receiver. The higher the terminal and the greater the space encompassed by the wires, the more pronounced is the effect, but it must be understood that it is purely local and has little to do with the real trouble.

In 1900, while perfecting my wireless system, one form of apparatus compressed four antennae. These were carefully calibrated in the same frequency and connected in multiple with the object of magnifying the action in receiving from any direction. When I desired to ascertain the origin of the transmitted impulse, each diagonally situated pair was put in series with a primary coil energizing the detector circuit. In the former case, the sound was loud in the telephone; in the latter it ceased, as expected, the two antennae neutralizing each other, but the true static manifested themselves in both instances and I had to devise special preventives embodying different principles. By employing receivers connected to two points of the ground, as suggested by me long ago, this trouble caused by the charged air, which is very serious in the structures as now built, is nullified and besides, the liability of all kinds of interference is reduced to about one-half because of the directional character of the circuit. This was perfectly self-evident, but came as a revelation to some simple-minded wireless folks whose experience was confined to forms of apparatus that could have been improved with an axe, and they have been disposing of the bear's skin before killing him. If it were true that strays performed such antics, it would be easy to get rid of them by receiving without aerials. But, as a matter of fact, a wire buried in the ground which, conforming to this view, should be absolutely immune, is more susceptible to certain extraneous impulses than one placed vertically in the air. To state it fairly, a slight progress has been made, but not by virtue of any particular method or device. It was achieved simply by discerning the enormous structures, which are bad enough for transmission but wholly unsuitable for reception and adopting a more appropriate type of receiver. As I have said before, to dispose of this difficulty for good, a radical change must be made in the system and the sooner this is done the better.

It would be calamitous, indeed, if at this time when the art is in its infancy and the vast majority, not excepting even experts, have no conception of its ultimate possibilities, a measure would be rushed through the legislature making it a government monopoly. This was proposed a few weeks ago by Secretary Daniel's and no doubt that distinguished official has made his appeal to the Senate and House of Representatives with sincere conviction. But universal evidence unmistakably shows that the best results are always obtained in healthful commercial competition. there are, however, exceptional reasons why wireless should be given the fullest freedom of development. In the first place, it offers prospects immeasurably greater and more vital to betterment of human life than any other invention or discovery in the history of man. Then again, it must be understood that this wonderful art has been, in its entirety, evolved here and can be called "American" with more right and propriety than the telephone, the incandescent lamp or the airplane.

Enterprising press agents and stock jobbers have been so successful in spreading misinformation, that even so excellent a periodical as the "Scientific American," accords the chief credit to a foreign country. The Germans, of course, gave us the Hertz waves and the Russian, English, French and Italian experts were quick in using them for signaling purposes. It was an obvious application of the new agent and accomplished with the old classical and unimproved induction coil, scarcely anything more than another kind of heliography. The radius of transmission was very limited, the result attained of little value, and the Hertz oscillations, as a means for conveying intelligence, could have been advantageously replaced by sound waves, which I advocated in 1891. Moreover, all of these attempts were made three years after the basic principles of the wireless system, which is universally employed today, and its potent instrumentalities had been clearly described and developed in America.

No trace of those Hertzian appliances and methods remains today. We have proceeded in the very opposite direction and what has been done is the product of the brains and efforts of citizens of this country. The fundamental patents have expired and the opportunities are open to all. The chief argument of the Secretary is based on interference. According to his statement, reported in the New York Herald of July 29th, signals from a powerful station can be intercepted in every village in the world. In view of this fact, which was demonstrated in my experiments in 1900, it would be of little use to impose restrictions in the United States.

As throwing light on this point, I may mention that only recently an odd looking gentleman called on me with the object of enlisting my services in the construction of world transmitters in some distant land. "We have no money," he said, "but carloads of solid gold, and we will give you a liberal amount." I told him that I wanted to see first what will be done with my inventions in America, and this ended the interview. But I am satisfied that some dark forces are at work, and as time goes on the maintenance of continuous communication will be rendered more difficult. The only remedy is a system immune against interruption. It has been perfected, it exists, and all that is necessary is to put it in operation.

The terrible conflict is still uppermost in the minds and perhaps the greatest importance will be attached to the Magnifying Transmitter as a machine for attack and defense, more particularly in connection with TELAUTAMATICS. This invention is a logical outcome of observations begun in my boyhood and continued throughout my life. When the first results were published, the Electrical Review stated editorially that it would become one of the "most potent factors in the advance of civilization of mankind." The time is not distant when this prediction will be fulfilled. In 1898 and 1900, it was offered by me to the Government and might have been adopted, were I one of those who would go to Alexander's shepherd when they want a favor from Alexander! At that time I really thought that it would abolish war, because of its unlimited destructiveness and exclusion of the personal element of combat. But while I have not lost faith in its potentialities, my views have changed since. War can not be avoided until the physical cause for its recurrence is removed and this, in the last analysis, is the vast extent of the planet on which we live. Only though annihilation of distance in every respect, as the conveyance of intelligence, transport of passengers and supplies and transmission of energy will conditions be brought about some day, insuring permanency of friendly relations. What we now want most is closer contact and better understanding between individuals and communities all over the earth and the elimination of that fanatic devotion to exalted ideals of national egoism and pride, which is always prone to plunge the world into primeval barbarism and strife. No league or parliamentary act of any kind will ever prevent such a calamity. These are only new devices for putting the weak at the mercy of the strong.

I have expressed myself in this regard fourteen years ago, when a combination of a few leading governments, a sort of Holy alliance, was advocated by the late Andrew Carnegie, who may be fairly considered as the father of this idea, having given to it more publicity and impetus than anybody else prior to the efforts of the President. While it can not be denied that such aspects might be of material advantage to some less fortunate peoples, it can not attain the chief objective sought. Peace can only come as a natural consequence of universal enlightenment and merging of races, and we are still far from this blissful realization, because few indeed, will admit the reality that God made man in His image in which case all earth men are alike. There is in fact but one race, of many colors. Christ is but one person, yet he is of all people, so why do some people think themselves better than some other people?

As I view the world of today, in the light of the gigantic struggle we have witnessed, I am filled with conviction that the interests of humanity would be best served if the United States remained true to its traditions, true to God whom it pretends to believe, and kept out of "entangling alliances." Situated as it is, geographically remote from the theaters of impending conflicts, without incentive to territorial aggrandizement, with inexhaustible resources and immense population thoroughly imbued with the spirit of liberty and right, this country is placed in a unique and privileged position. It is thus able to exert, independently, its colossal strength and moral force to the benefit of all, more judiciously and effectively, than as a member of a league.

I have dwelt on the circumstances of my early life and told of an affliction which compelled me to unremitting exercise of imagination and self-observation. This mental activity, at first involuntary under the pressure of illness and suffering, gradually became second nature and led me finally to recognize that I was but an automaton devoid of free will in thought and action and merely responsible to the forces of the environment. Our bodies are of such complexity of structure, the motions we perform are so numerous and involved and the external impressions on our sense organs to such a degree delicate and elusive, that it is hard for the average person to grasp this fact. Yet nothing is more convincing to the trained investigator than the mechanistic theory of life which had been, in a measure, understood and propounded by Descartes three hundred years ago. In his time many important functions of our organisms were unknown and especially with respect to the nature of light and the construction and operation of the eye, philosophers were in the dark.

In recent years the progress of scientific research in these fields has been such as to leave no room for a doubt in regard to this view on which many works have been published. One of its ablest and most eloquent exponents is, perhaps, Felix le Dantec, formerly assistant of Pasteur. Professor Jacques Loeb has performed remarkable experiments in heliotropism, clearly establishing the controlling power of light in lower forms of organisms and his latest book, "Forced Movements," is revelatory. But while men of science accept this theory simply as any other that is recognized, to me it is a truth which I hourly demonstrate by every act and thought of mine. The consciousness of the external impression prompting me to any kind of exertion, physical or mental, is ever present in my mind. Only on very rare occasions, when I was in a state of exceptional concentration, have I found difficulty in locating the original impulse. The by far greater number of human beings are never aware of what is passing around and within them and millions fall victims of disease and die prematurely just on this account. The commonest, everyday occurrences appear to them mysterious and inexplicable. One may feel a sudden wave of sadness and rack his brain for an explanation, when he might have noticed that it was caused by a cloud cutting off the rays of the sun. He may see the image of a friend dear to him under conditions which he construes as very peculiar, when only shortly before he has passed him in the street or seen his photograph somewhere. When he loses a collar button, he fusses and swears for an hour, being unable to visualize his previous actions and locate the object directly. Deficient observation is merely a form of ignorance and responsible for the many morbid notions and foolish ideas prevailing. There is not more than one out of every ten persons who does not believe in telepathy and other psychic manifestations, spiritualism and communion with the dead, and who would refuse to listen to willing or unwilling deceivers?

Just to illustrate how deeply rooted this tendency has become even among the clear-headed American population, I may mention a comical incident. Shortly before the war, when the exhibition of my turbines in this city elicited widespread comment in the technical papers, I anticipated that there would be a scramble among manufacturers to get hold of the invention and I had particular designs on that man from Detroit who has an uncanny faculty for accumulating millions. So confident was I, that he would turn up some day, that I declared this as certain to my secretary and assistants. Sure enough, one fine morning a body of engineers from the Ford Motor Company presented themselves with the request of discussing with me an important project. "Didn't I tell you?" I remarked triumphantly to my employees, and one of them said, "You are amazing, Mr. Tesla. Everything comes out exactly as you predict."

As soon as these hardheaded men were seated, I of course, immediately began to extol the wonderful features of my turbine, when the spokesman interrupted me and said, "We know all about this, but we are on a special errand. We have formed a psychological society for the investigation of psychic phenomena and we want you to join us in this undertaking." I suppose these engineers never knew how near they came to being fired out of my office. Ever since I was told by some of the greatest men of the time, leaders in science whose names are immortal, that I am possessed of an unusual mind, I bent all my thinking faculties on the solution of great problems regardless of sacrifice. For many years I endeavoured to solve the enigma of death, and watched eagerly for every kind of spiritual indication. But only once in the course of my existence have I had an experience which momentarily impressed me as supernatural. It was at the time of my mother's death. I had become completely exhausted by pain and long vigilance, and one night was carried to a building about two blocks from our home. As I lay helpless there, I thought that if my mother died while I was away from her bedside, she would surely give me a sign. Two or three months before, I was in London in company with my late friend, Sir William Crookes, when spiritualism was discussed and I was under the full sway of these thoughts. I might not have paid attention to other men, but was susceptible to his arguments as it was his epochal work on radiant matter, which I had read as a student, that made me embrace the electrical career. I reflected that the conditions for a look into the beyond were most favorable, for my mother was a woman of genius and particularly excelling in the powers of intuition. During the whole night every fibber in my brain was strained in expectancy, but nothing happened until early in the morning, when I fell in a sleep, or perhaps a swoon, and saw a cloud carrying angelic figures of marvelous beauty, one of whom gazed upon me lovingly and gradually assumed the features of my mother. The appearance slowly floated across the room and vanished, and I was awakened by an indescribably sweet song of many voices. In that instant a certitude, which no words can express, came upon me that my mother had just died. And that was true. I was unable to understand the tremendous weight of the painful knowledge I received in advance, and wrote a letter to Sir William Crookes while still under the domination of these impressions and in poor bodily health. When I recovered, I sought for a long time the external cause of this strange manifestation and, to my great relief, I succeeded after many months of fruitless effort.

I had seen the painting of a celebrated artist, representing allegorically one of the seasons in the form of a cloud with a group of angels which seemed to actually float in the air, and this had struck me forcefully. It was exactly the same that appeared in my dream, with the exception of my mother's likeness. The music came from the choir in the church nearby at the early mass of Easter morning, explaining everything satisfactorily in conformity with scientific facts. This occurred long ago, and I have never had the faintest reason since to change my views on psychical and spiritual phenomena, for which there is no foundation. The belief in these is the natural outgrowth of intellectual development. Religious dogmas are no longer accepted in their orthodox meaning, but every individual clings to faith in a supreme power of some kind.

We all must have an ideal to govern our conduct and insure contentment, but it is immaterial whether it be one of creed, art, science, or anything else, so long as it fulfills the function of a dematerializing force. It is essential to the peaceful existence of humanity as a whole that one common conception should prevail. While I have failed to obtain any evidence in support of the contentions of psychologists and spiritualists, I have proved to my complete satisfaction the automatism of life, not only through continuous observations of individual actions, but even more conclusively through certain generalizations. these amount to a discovery which I consider of the greatest moment to human society, and on which I shall briefly dwell.

I got the first inkling of this astonishing truth when I was still a very young man, but for many years I interpreted what I noted simply as coincidences. Namely, whenever either myself or a person to whom I was attached, or a cause to which I was devoted, was hurt by others in a particular way, which might be best popularly characterized as the most unfair imaginable, I experienced a singular and undefinable pain which, for the want of a better term, I have qualified as "cosmic" and shortly thereafter, and invariably, those who had inflicted it came to grief. After many such cases I confided this to a number of friends, who had the opportunity to convince themselves of the theory of which I have gradually formulated and which may be stated in the following few words: Our bodies are of similar construction and exposed to the same external forces. This results in likeness of response and concordance of the general activities on which all our social and other rules and laws are based. We are automata entirely controlled by the forces of the medium, being tossed about like corks on the surface of the water, but mistaking the resultant of the impulses from the outside for the free will. The movements and other actions we perform are always life preservative and though seemingly quite independent from one another, we are connected by invisible links. So long as the organism is in perfect order, it responds accurately to the agents that prompt it, but the moment that there is some derangement in any individual, his self-preservative power is impaired.

Everybody understands, of course, that if one becomes deaf, has his eyes weakened, or his limbs injured, the chances for his continued existence are lessened. But this is also true, and perhaps more so, of certain defects in the brain which drive the automaton, more or less, of that vital quality and cause it to rush into destruction. A very sensitive and observant being, with his highly developed mechanism all intact, and acting with precision in obedience to the changing conditions of the environment, is endowed with a transcending mechanical sense, enabling him to evade perils too subtle to be directly perceived. When he comes in contact with others whose controlling organs are radically faulty, that sense asserts itself and he feels the "cosmic" pain.

The truth of this has been borne out in hundreds of instances and I am inviting other students of nature to devote attention to this subject, believing that through combined systematic effort, results of incalculable value to the world will be attained. The idea of constructing an automaton, to bear out my theory, presented itself to me early, but I did not begin active work until 1895, when I started my wireless investigations. During the succeeding two or three years, a number of automatic mechanisms, to be actuated from a distance, were constructed by me and exhibited to visitors in my laboratory. In 1896, however, I designed a complete machine capable of a multitude of operations, but the consummation of my labours was delayed until late in 1897. This machine was illustrated and described in my article in the Century Magazine of June, 1900; and other periodicals of that time and when first shown in the beginning of 1898, it created a sensation such as no other invention of mine has ever produced. In November, 1898, a basic patent on the novel art was granted to me, but only after the Examiner-in-Chief had come to New York and witnessed the performance, for what I claimed seemed unbelievable. I remember that when later I called on an official in Washington, with a view of offering the invention to the Government, he burst out in laughter upon my telling him what I had accomplished. Nobody thought then that there was the faintest prospect of perfecting such a device. It is unfortunate that in this patent, following the advice of my attorneys, I indicated the control as being affected through the medium of a single circuit and a well-known form of detector, for the reason that I had not yet secured protection on my methods and apparatus for individualization. As a matter of fact, my boats were controlled through the joint action of several circuits and interference of every kind was excluded.

Most generally, I employed receiving circuits in the form of loops, including condensers, because the discharges of my high-tension transmitter ionized the air in the (laboratory) so that even a very small aerial would draw electricity from the surrounding atmosphere for hours. Just to give an idea, I found, for instance, that a bulb twelve inches in diameter, highly exhausted, and with one single terminal to which a short wire was attached, would deliver well on to one thousand successive flashes before all charge of the air in the laboratory was neutralized. The loop form of receiver was not sensitive to such a disturbance and it is curious to note that it is becoming popular at this late date. In reality, it collects much less energy than the aerials or a long grounded wire, but it so happens that it does away with a number of defects inherent to the present wireless devices.

In demonstrating my invention before audiences, the visitors were requested to ask questions, however involved, and the automaton would answer them by signs. This was considered magic at the time, but was extremely simple, for it was myself who gave the replies by means of the device. At the same period, another larger telautomatic boat was constructed, a photograph of which was shown in the October 1919 number of the Electrical Experimenter. It was controlled by loops, having several turns placed in the hull, which was made entirely watertight and capable of submergence. The apparatus was similar to that used in the first with the exception of certain special features I introduced as, for example, incandescent lamps which afforded a visible evidence of the proper functioning of the machine. These automata, controlled within the range of vision of the operator, were, however, the first and rather crude steps in the evolution of the art of Telautomatics as I had conceived it.

The next logical improvement was its application to automatic mechanisms beyond the limits of vision and at great distances from the center of control, and I have ever since advocated their employment as instruments of warfare in preference to guns. The importance of this now seems to be recognized, if I am to judge from casual announcements through the press, of achievements which are said to be extraordinary but contain no merit of novelty, whatever. In an imperfect manner it is practicable, with the existing wireless plants, to launch an airplane, have it follow a certain approximate course, and perform some operation at a distance of many hundreds of miles. A machine of this kind can also be mechanically controlled in several ways and I have no doubt that it may prove of some usefulness in war. But there are to my best knowledge, no instrumentalities in existence today with which such an object could be accomplished in a precise manner. I have devoted years of study to this matter and have evolved means, making such and greater wonders easily realizable.

As stated on a previous occasion, when I was a student at college I conceived a flying machine quite unlike the present ones.

The underlying principle was sound, but could not be carried into practice for want of a prime-mover of sufficiently great activity. In recent years, I have successfully solved this problem and am now planning aerial machines *devoid of sustaining planes, ailerons, propellers, and other external* attachments, which will be capable of immense speeds and are very likely to furnish powerful arguments for peace in the near future. Such a machine, sustained and propelled "entirely by reaction," is shown on one of the pages of my lectures, and is supposed to be controlled either mechanically, or by wireless energy. By installing proper plants, it will be practicable to "project a missile of this kind into the air and drop it" almost on the very spot designated, which may be thousands of miles away.

But we are not going to stop at this. Telautomats will be ultimately produced, capable of acting as if possessed of their own intelligence, and their advent will create a revolution. As early as 1898, I proposed to representatives of a large manufacturing concern the construction and public exhibition of an automobile carriage which, left to itself, would perform a great variety of operations involving something akin to judgment. But my proposal was deemed chimerical at the time and nothing came of it. At present, many of the ablest minds are trying to devise expedients for preventing a repetition of the awful conflict which is only theoretically ended and the duration and main issues of which I have correctly predicted in an article printed in the SUN of December 20, 1914. The proposed League is not a remedy but, on the contrary, in the opinion of a number of competent men, may bring about results just the opposite.

It is particularly regrettable that a punitive policy was adopted in framing the terms of peace, because a few years hence, it will be possible for nations to fight without armies, ships or guns, by weapons far more terrible, to the destructive action and range of which there is virtually no limit. Any city, at a distance, whatsoever, from the enemy, can be destroyed by him and no power on earth can stop him from doing so. If we want to avert an impending calamity and a state of things which may transform the globe into an inferno, we should push the development of flying machines and wireless transmission of energy without an instant's delay and with all the power and resources of the nation.

The Man Behind the Mind

IN the small village of Smiljan, Croatia (then Austria-Hungary), Nikola Tesla was born exactly at the stroke of midnight between July 9 and 10, 1856 -- an incidental schism that befits the beginnings of a man who always seemed out of time with the world around him.

From early childhood, it was apparent that Nikola possessed an extraordinary mind. His father, Milutin Tesla, was a minister who trained Nikola to strengthen his memory and reasoning skills through a variety of regular mental exercises. But Tesla gave the highest credit for his talents to his mother's side of the family, whom he referred to as a long line of inventors. Despite Djouka Tesla's lack of formal education, she created numerous original tools for sewing and other tasks around her household.

Tesla had an older brother, Dane, whom he considered his superior in every way. When Nikola was five and Dane was twelve, Nikola was jealous of Dane's white stallion, which their father said Nikola was too young to ride. One day Nikola used a blow gun to shoot a pea at the horse, causing it to throw Dane from its back. Dane later died from his injuries. Feelings of guilt over this tragedy haunted Tesla throughout his life. No matter how great his achievements, he always believed that Dane could have outdone him.

During his early life, Tesla was stricken with illness time and time again. He suffered a peculiar affliction in which blinding flashes of light would appear before his eyes, often accompanied by hallucinations. Much of the time the visions were linked to a word or idea he might come across; just by hearing the name of an item, he would involuntarily envision it in realistic detail. The flashes and images caused Tesla great discomfort, and by the time he reached his teens he had taught himself to repress them from occurring except in certain times of stress. When they did happen, they sometimes had a nature that might be described as psychic.

In one case, the young Tesla recklessly attempted to swim beneath a large floating structure that extended further than he realized. Finding himself trapped in the dark water with no sign of the surface, a flash appeared, and with it a vision of a small opening to air. Tesla's vision turned out to be correct, and the strange curse apparently saved him from drowning. Upon the deaths of his father and mother, Tesla claimed to have detailed premonitions just before each passing. In his later years, Tesla boasted of successfully transmitting an image from his mind into that of a person in another room.

Shortly after his graduation from high school, Tesla suffered a devastating bout with cholera and nearly died. He was bedridden for nine months, and doctors announced that he would not live much longer. Tesla was occupying his still-active mind by reading as much as his body would permit, when he encountered a strange new kind of literature: "Innocents Abroad," by Mark Twain. Tesla was captivated by the humor and humanity of this up-and-coming American author, whose work so raised his spirits that he made a miraculously abrupt recovery to health. Years later in the United States, Tesla met Samuel Clemens and was able to thank him for having saved his life. Clemens went on to become one of Tesla's few close friends.

Tesla underwent another debilitating trauma a few years after recovering from cholera. This time, the nature of the illness and its causes were a complete mystery. Tesla's physical senses, which had always been remarkably acute, seemed to go inexplicably into overdrive, paralyzing him with an overabundance of sensation. The ticking of a pocket watch had become painfully deafening to him, even from several rooms away. He needed rubber cushion inserted beneath the feet of his bed to lessen the vibrations from outside passersby, which felt to him like an earthquake. Exposure to light was excruciating not only for his eyes, but to the surface of his skin, as well. After a time, the crippling condition eased, and Tesla returned to normal sensory perception with a mental breakthrough that led him to the invention of the alternating current motor.

The physical and emotional travails of Tesla's early life undoubtedly helped shape him into the singular man he was: a man of immense brilliance, and a nearly equal level of eccentricity. Tesla shunned physical contact with other people, with a special aversion to touching hair. To avoid shaking hands with people he met, he lied that he had injured his hands in a laboratory accident. He apparently never took part in a romantic relationship of any kind. A female acquaintance who grew enamored of Tesla reportedly once took the initiative to kiss him, causing the startled inventor to flee in agony. Still, Tesla exhibited some appreciation for feminine beauty by demanding that his secretaries conform to an exacting standard of dress and physique. His female employees were forbidden to wear pearls, which Tesla for some reason found hideously repulsive.

Other behaviors of Tesla's seemed to drift into the realm of compulsive-obsessive disorder. He required any repeated actions in his daily life (such as the footsteps he took in a walk) to be divisible by three, and would keep repeating them until he arrived at a suitable total. Quantities of twenty-seven were the most prized of all, since that number was three cubed. Tesla also felt compelled to calculate the exact volume of his food before he ate it. This involved measuring his meal portions with a ruler and dipping pieces in water to determine how many cubic centimeters they displaced. He was especially fond of saltine crackers because of their uniformity of volume. Many times, such as during the heat of a major project, Tesla would forget to eat altogether, and work for days without sleep. At one point his all-consuming devotion to the laboratory brought on an exhaustion so severe that for several days he lost all memory of who he was.

Tesla asserted that it was not until he reached adulthood that he discovered he was an inventor. He discounted his early years (perhaps unreasonably) as a time of undisciplined impulses, entirely lacking focus. But he did invent a wide array of creations and schemes as a child. The first was a simple hook-and-line device for catching frogs. All his young friends imitated it, and the mechanisms performed so well that the local frog population was nearly eradicated. He also built a miniature water wheel which was unique in that it propelled itself without blades. This memory would later inspire his innovation of the bladeless turbine.

The young Tesla created a remarkable machine powered by another natural energy source: June bugs (or, as Europeans call them, May bugs). He glued sixteen of the live insects to the blades of a small windmill-like structure, and they set the rotor spinning vigorously in their vain attempt to fly away. Some accounts have jokingly cited this effort as one of Tesla's rare failures, although the inventor himself remained rather proud of the June bug motor. In his autobiography, Tesla explained why he discontinued his research into insect energy:

"These creatures were remarkably efficient, for once they were started, they had no sense to stop and continued whirling for hours and hours and the hotter it was, the harder they worked. All went well until a strange boy came to the place. He was the son of a retired officer in the Austrian army. That urchin ate May-bugs alive and enjoyed them as though they were the finest blue-point oysters."

Adding one more entry to his long list of idiosyncrasies, after beholding that spectacle Tesla refused ever to touch another insect again.

The Fight for AC

Tesla began his college education at Graz Polytechnic Institute, pursuing studies of the topic that fascinated him above all others: electricity. He had done fairly well in grade school, but his lack of facility at freehand drawing kept him from excelling in technical courses. But in college, Tesla was delighted to find, he was permitted to focus exclusively on what he was best at.

He studied feverishly almost around the clock, in a routine that began at 3 a.m. and ended at 11 p.m., every day. He aimed to impress his parents with his scholarly achievements, in part because his father had been reluctant to send him to the university, wishing Nikola would follow in his footsteps in the clergy. He also entertained fantasies of going to America and teaming up with the reigning leader of electrical invention, Thomas Edison, so that their combined forces might revolutionize the world.

Tesla was an extraordinary student who frequently enraged his professors, questioning the technological status quo with an insight that surpassed his instructors'. He rebelled most stringently against the acceptance of direct current as the sole means of delivering electrical power. It was plain to him that DC was inefficient and incapable of adequately transmitting power over long distances, and there had to be a better way. There was talk of a theoretical "alternating current" system, but no one had figured out how to make it work. AC was frowned upon as a fanciful dream by the scientific establishment, in much the same way as cold fusion is regarded today. Tesla's merest suggestion of AC brought scorn in his lecture halls, but he was never discouraged enough to abandon the enticing riddle.

In the middle of Tesla's sophomore year of college, his father was felled by a stroke. Nikola returned home, and his father died soon after. Tesla never returned to the Polytechnic Institute. Lacking funds for tuition, he took a job at a government telegraph office.

Tesla despaired for his interrupted education, but held on to his dream of becoming an electrical pioneer.

It was at this time that Tesla endured his ordeal with hypersensitivity that reduced him to a bedridden invalid. Considering the depressing turns his life had just taken, the bizarre affliction could possibly have been psychosomatic in origin. Whatever its cause, when Tesla finally emerged from the prolonged fugue state, he was armed with a powerful new insight on how alternating current could be successfully attained.

His great mental leap was this: two coils positioned at right angles and supplied with alternating current 90 out of phase could make a magnetic field rotate, with no need for the cumbersome commutator used in direct current motors. Tesla knew it would work without even having to build it and test it. Constructing it mentally and letting it run in his mind was proof enough for him.

This was Tesla's method for developing inventions throughout his career: no journals, no blueprints, no prototypes. The propensity for turning ideas into concrete visualizations which had tormented him in his youth was now turned to Tesla's advantage. He believed his technique was not only a valid one, but actually superior to the common practice of getting everything down on paper and conducting tentative trials. "The moment one constructs a device to carry into practice a crude idea, he finds himself unavoidably engrossed with the details of the apparatus," Tesla wrote in his autobiography. "As he goes on improving and reconstructing, his force of concentration diminishes and he loses sight of the great underlying principle."

Tesla now possessed the answer, but the problem of putting it into practice remained. In 1882 he found employment with Continental Edison Company in Paris, distinguishing himself as a fine engineer. Two years later he traveled to New York to meet the company's president, Thomas Edison himself.

It was not the harmonious meeting of the minds Tesla had once dreamed of. Edison regarded the hotshot European with contempt, and assuredly held no intentions of collaborating with him on some harebrained AC scheme. Edison viewed AC as a pipe dream at best, or, at worst, a threat to usurp his DC-based empire.

Tesla tried to make the best of the situation by offering to improve Edison's existing technology to the highest level possible.

He promised to increase the efficiency of the DC dynamos by 25%, within two months' time. The skeptical Edison said he would pay Tesla fifty thousand dollars if he succeeded.

Exerting a massive, virtually non-stop effort, Tesla accomplished the feat, enhancing the dynamos by an even better margin than he proposed. But when he asked for his fifty thousand dollars, Edison refused to honor the deal, claiming that he had only been joking. Infuriated, Tesla quit and never worked for Edison again.

Tesla was soon approached by a group of investors who wished to market the arc lamp he had developed. Thus was the Tesla Electric Company founded. Tesla was eager to seize this opportunity to bring AC into existence at last, but his investors wanted nothing to do with it -- so Tesla found himself rejected by the company that bore his own name.

That company soon ran afoul of financial hardships, leaving Tesla's stock shares worthless and stripping him of his rights to the arc light. Penniless, his enterprising spirit finally broken, one of the world's most brilliant men was reduced to shoveling in a labor crew for a dollar a day. He planned on committing suicide on his upcoming thirtieth birthday, at the stroke of midnight.

Before that could happen, A. K. Brown of Western Union learned of Tesla's plight. Aghast, Brown was determined to restore the genius to a worthy place, and offered to furnish him with a laboratory of his own. And what's more, Brown wanted Tesla to pursue the possibilities of alternating current.

Granted a blessed salvation, Tesla immediately went to work assembling his AC dynamo at last. It functioned in reality precisely as it had all those years inside his head. Tesla demonstrated his invention in a heavily publicized lecture, and instantly became the toast of the engineering community.

Among the AC converts in the lecture's audience was George Westinghouse, who negotiated with Tesla to manufacture the dynamos. The first application of the new technology: Niagara Falls. Westinghouse won the coveted contract to harness Niagara, bidding half of what Edison bid for the installation of a DC system. In 1895, the Niagara AC power system enjoyed a flawless inauguration, transmitting electricity to Buffalo twenty-two miles away – a complete impossibility in the suddenly outmoded world of direct current. No longer a curious luxury reserved for the urban upper class, electric power in the home would now be commonplace.

For the first time in his life, Nikola Tesla was an indisputable success.

Free Energy

From the beginning of A. K. Brown's and George Westinghouse's fortuitous partnerships with Tesla, the inventor was at work on other projects above and beyond the AC dynamo. Able to devote himself to the unhindered realization of his countless ideas, he would later recall these years of his life as "little short of continuous rapture."

Tesla's New York laboratory was a hive of continuous activity, with a small staff of assistants working solely from their employer's verbal instructions. His distaste for putting ideas down on paper, coupled with his tendency to get bored with a completed invention and move on to the next challenge, led Tesla to toss aside a large number of creations that he never even bothered to patent. Once, when exhaustion left Tesla in a state of temporary amnesia, his assistant filed for patents on many of the unregistered inventions on Tesla's behalf, and had the master sign the papers while still incapacitated. Tesla's shunning of documentation was of some benefit when fire destroyed the lab in 1895, right after the success at Niagara. The loss was a setback, but not a catastrophic one, since the most valuable of the laboratory's assets remained intact in Tesla's brain.

In 1891, Tesla developed the invention by which his name is most commonly known today: the Tesla coil. Simple enough for today's hobbyists and science-fair entrants to construct in fully functional homemade models, it was nonetheless a remarkable innovation which remains the basis for radios, televisions and other modern means of wireless communication.

Tesla became known for the lectures at which he demonstrated his inventions and concepts with a theatrical flair. Many attendees were laymen who had little comprehension of what Tesla said, but were mesmerized by the bolts of lightning that leapt from his ominously humming coils, and the unwired light bulbs that lit at the touch of Tesla's hand. These spectacular displays led

Tesla to be popularly regarded as some sort of magician -- a title that was bestowed not in ridicule, but in awe.

The wireless transmission of energy would become the ultimate pursuit of Tesla's career. He discovered that a vacuum tube held in proximity to a Tesla coil would burst into illumination, without wires, without even a filament inside the glowing tube. Electrical resonance was the key to this discovery. By determining the frequency of the needed electrical current, Tesla was able to turn a series of different lights on and off selectively, from yards away. He had just become an American citizen in 1891, and this new technology was to be his gift of thanks to his adoptive country: a means of transmitting energy instantly, across any distance, through thin air. Free energy for everyone.

One of Tesla's assistants reportedly questioned the implications of putting such an energy distribution plan into practice. He wondered what incentive there would be for the electrical power establishment to begin giving away its goods for free, and whether Tesla could possibly be "allowed" to introduce such an arrangement. The presence of such doubts enraged Tesla, who was convinced, somewhat naively, that his plan would be accepted simply because it was the right thing to do.

As the years passed, Tesla's vision of wireless energy grew even grander in scope. He solved one of the problems implicit in his first theory, which was that transmission of power through air over long distances would result in a significant loss of energy. Rather than using air as a medium, he decided to send energy through the ground. This makes little sense in conventional electrical terms, whereby the earth's surface is regarded as, literally, "the ground" – a sinkhole used for discharging excess current from a conductor. But Tesla found that if it were charged highly enough, the ground could become the conductor itself. In this way, the entire planet could be transformed into a colossal electric transmitter.

In 1899, as logistics prevented him from conducting the necessary experiments within the confines of New York City, Tesla headed west. A Colorado attorney named Leonard Curtis, who had previously defended Tesla in court, offered to help Tesla set up a testing facility in Colorado Springs. Curtis was also an officer of the local power company, and provided electricity to Tesla at no cost.

Tesla and his assistants built a one-of-a-kind laboratory on the outskirts of town, which looked like a large barn topped by a 180-foot metal tower. This was Tesla's "magnifying transformer," which he called the greatest of his inventions.

The townspeople of Colorado Springs were naturally curious about what this great inventor was up to, and respected the signs around the perimeter of the compound reading "KEEP OUT – GREAT DANGER!" Still, they soon felt the effects of Tesla's apparatus. Sparks leapt from the ground as people walked the streets, singeing their feet through their shoes. The grass around the Tesla building glowed with a faint blue light. Metal objects held near fire hydrants would draw miniature lightning bolts from several inches away. Switched-off light bulbs within 100 feet of the tower spontaneously lit.

And Tesla was only tuning up his equipment. These were the side effects of adjusting the magnifying transformer into perfect resonance with the earth. Once it was properly calibrated, Tesla was ready to conduct his career's boldest symphony, using the entire planet as his orchestra.

Late one night in the fall of 1899, Tesla fired up his machine at full blast, in hopes of producing a phenomenon he called resonant rise. His tower pumped ten million volts into the earth's surface. The current raced through the earth at the speed of light, powerful enough to keep from dying out over the course of its journey. When it reached the opposite side of the planet, it bounced back, like ripples of water returning to their origin. Upon returning, the current was greatly weakened; but Tesla was sending out a series of pulses which reinforced one another, resulting in a tremendous cumulative effect.

At ground zero, where Tesla and his assistant stood bedazzled, the resonant rise manifested itself in an unearthly display of lightning that still stands as the most powerful man-made electrical surge in history. The returning current formed an arc of lightning that stretched skyward from Tesla's tower and progressively grew to an incredible 130 feet long. Apocalyptic crashes of thunder were heard twenty-two miles away. Tesla had been concerned that there might be an upper limit to generating resonant surges, but now he believed the potential was limitless. The demonstration did come to an unexpected halt, but that was because the power surge caused the overloaded Colorado Springs power generator to burst into flames. Tesla received no further free power from the plant's furious owners.

He returned to New York in search of backing for the global implementation of a resonant energy system. Now cognizant of the business world's inevitable reluctance to support giving away free energy, Tesla pitched his new project as a means of transmitting communication, rather than electrical power. Decades before the birth of the Internet, Tesla was envisioning an information superhighway that was a far more sophisticated communication network than the one we use today.

George Westinghouse passed on the idea. Tesla next proposed it to J. P. Morgan, the wealthiest man in America, who had previously declined to finance the inventor. The idea of a monopoly on world communications intrigued Morgan, and he enabled Tesla to build a new laboratory on Long Island. Named Wardenclyffe, it was to be a bigger and better version of his Colorado facility.

While Tesla worked on the project, a string of accidents and bad luck struck Wardenclyffe, and he was beginning to run out of money. Morgan's funds and enthusiasm seemed to evaporate. In a last-ditch effort to keep his investor from deserting him, Tesla revealed to Morgan that his true goal was not to replace the telegraph, but to replace the conventional transmission of electricity. Morgan responded by withdrawing his support entirely.

Tesla would never get another opportunity to bring free energy to the world.

Tesla's Death Ray

Given that Tesla's inventions generally possessed an element of social conscience, of doing good for humanity, it may seem surprising that he created a number of devices with military applications. And the notion of the Tesla harnessing his mind for purposes of war may seem immensely frightening. After all, this is the man who boasted that with his resonance generator he could split the earth in two... and no one was ever quite sure whether he was joking.

The first Tesla invention with a proposed military use was his automaton technology, with which the labor of human beings could be performed by machines. Specifically, Tesla produced remote-controlled boats and submarines. He demonstrated the wireless ship at an exposition in Madison Square Garden in 1898. The automaton apparatus was so advanced, it used a form of voice recognition to respond to the verbal commands of Tesla and volunteers from the audience.

In public, Tesla spoke only of the humanitarian virtues of the invention: it would lessen the toils and drudgery of mankind and keep human lives out of harm's way. But Tesla actually had his hopes on a contract with the U.S. military. In a presentation before the War Department, Tesla argued that his unmanned torpedo craft could obliterate the Spanish Armada and end the war with Spain in an afternoon. The government never took Tesla up on his offer.

Tesla then decided to pitch the automated submarine to private industry, and submitted it for the approval of J. P. Morgan. According to some accounts, Morgan offered to manufacture Tesla's vessels, but only if Tesla would agree to marry Morgan's daughter. Such a deal was of course anathema to Tesla, and he and Morgan would not work together until Wardenclyffe, a couple of years later.

Tesla eventually landed a successful military contract -- with the German Marine High Command. The product here was not unmanned sea craft, but sophisticated turbines which Admiral von Tirpitz used to great success in his fleet of warships. After J. P. Morgan cut off his support of Wardenclyffe, this foreign contract was Tesla's only substantial source of income. Upon the outbreak of World War I, Tesla chose to forfeit his German royalties, lest he be charged with treason.

Nearly broke, and finding the United States on the brink of war, Tesla dreamed up a new invention that might interest the military: the death ray.

The mechanism behind Tesla's death ray is not well understood. It was apparently some sort of particle accelerator. Tesla said it was an outgrowth of his magnifying transformer, which focused its energy output into a thin beam so concentrated it would not scatter, even over huge distances. He promoted the device as a purely defensive weapon, intended to knock down incoming attacks, making the death ray the great-great grandfather of the Strategic Defense Initiative.

It is not certain if Tesla ever used the death ray, or indeed if he even succeeded in building one. But the following is the often-related story of what happened one night in 1908 when Tesla tested the foreboding weapon.

At the time, Robert Peary was making his second attempt to reach the North Pole. Cryptically, Tesla had notified the expedition that he would be trying to contact them somehow. They were to report to him the details of anything unusual they might witness on the open tundra. On the evening of June 30, accompanied by his associate George Scherff atop Wardenclyffe tower, Tesla aimed his death ray across the Atlantic towards the arctic, to a spot which he calculated was west of the Peary expedition.

Tesla switched on the device. At first, it was hard to tell if it was even working. Its extremity emitted a dim light that was barely visible. Then an owl flew from its perch on the tower's pinnacle, soaring into the path of the beam. The bird disintegrated instantly.

That concluded the test. Tesla watched the newspapers and sent telegrams to Peary in hopes of confirming the death ray's effectiveness. Nothing turned up. Tesla was ready to admit failure when news came of a strange event in Siberia.

On June 30, a massive explosion had devastated Tunguska, a remote area in the Siberian wilderness. Five hundred thousand square acres of land had been instantly destroyed. Equivalent to ten to fifteen megatons of TNT, the Tunguska incident is the most powerful explosion to have occurred in human history – not even subsequent thermonuclear detonations have surpassed it. The explosion was audible from 620 miles away. Scientists believe it was caused by either a meteorite or a fragment of a comet, although no obvious impact site or mineral remnants of such an object were ever found.

Nikola Tesla had a different explanation. It was plain that his death ray had overshot its intended target and destroyed Tunguska. He was thankful beyond measure that the explosion had—miraculously—killed no one. Tesla dismantled the death ray at once, deeming it too dangerous to remain in existence.

Six years later, the onset of the First World War caused Tesla to reconsider. He wrote to President Wilson, revealing his secret death ray test. He offered to rebuild the weapon for the War Department, to be used purely as a deterrent. The mere threat of such destructive force, he claimed, would cause the warring nations to agree at once to establish lasting peace.

The only response to Tesla's proposal was a form letter of appreciation from the president's secretary. The death ray was never reconstructed, and for that we should probably all be thankful.

Tesla made one one further attempt to aid in his country's war effort. In 1917, he conceived of a sending station that would emit exploratory waves of energy, enabling its operators to determine the precise location of distant enemy craft. The War Department rejected Tesla's "exploring ray" as a laughing stock.

A generation later, a new invention exactly like this helped the Allies win World War II. It was called radar.

His Wildest Dreams

Forever restless, and untethered by concerns of practicality and marketability, Tesla's mind spawned a vast miscellany of odd inventions. Many of these were never developed beyond the concept stage, and the ideas seemed to grow markedly weirder in the final years of Tesla's life. Invention was normally a deliberate process for Tesla, his every intention and goal fully formed before he and his crew lifted a finger. But there were times when he stumbled upon a new discovery by mistake.

Tesla performed his first experiments with resonance technology at his New York laboratory by firing up a small oscillator, which caused a minor amount of vibration. Suddenly, an alarmed squad of police officers stormed into the lab, demanding that Tesla stop at once. Manhattan was shaking for miles around. Tesla had not taken into account how resonance waves grow stronger the further they travel from their source. He had unintentionally created what became known as Tesla's earthquake machine.

Tesla also applied his resonance engines in bizarre forms of physical therapy. He created machines that flooded the human body with electrical currents and strong vibrations, intended to soothe aches and promote healing. And Tesla wasn't just the inventor of the "electrotherapeutic" device – he was also a client. He reportedly became somewhat addicted to administering the treatment to himself, insisting that a session with the machine rejuvenated him on his long stretches of work without food or sleep. Tesla once let his friend Samuel Clemens try out the healing machine. The author is said to have enjoyed the experience tremendously - until the vibrations brought him a case of spontaneous diarrhea. Tesla marketed this invention, and the Tesla Electrotherapeutic Company was one of the few commercial enterprises of his old age that was marginally successful.

Tesla gained another accidental revelation during his testing of the magnifying transformer in Colorado Springs. One evening during the construction of the device, the apparatus began to sound out a series of precise clicks, similar to Morse code. Tesla was convinced that these were signals being sent by extraterrestrial life. Tesla had expressed his belief in life on Mars, and now he thought he had proof. He later conceived of establishment of peaceful relations with our neighbors from outer space was among the most pressing duties that lay before humanity.

In his later years, Tesla was fascinated with the idea of light as both a particle and a wave - the fundamental proposition of what would become quantum physics. This field of inquiry led to the development of his death ray. Tesla also had the idea of creating a "wall of light" by manipulating electromagnetic waves in a certain pattern. This mysterious wall of light would enable time, space, gravity and matter to be altered at will, and engendered an array of Tesla proposals that seem to leap straight out of science fiction, including anti-gravity airships, teleportation and time travel.

The single weirdest invention Tesla ever proposed was probably the "thought photography" machine. He reasoned that a thought formed in the mind created a corresponding image in the retina, and the electrical data of this neural transmission could be read and recorded in a machine. The stored information could then be processed through an artificial optic nerve and played back as visual patterns on a view screen.

It is a pity Tesla never made this last invention a reality. With the dearth of written notes and documentation he left behind for modern science to study, we can only conclude that Tesla's weirdest ideas were misconceived fantasies - maybe even symptoms of madness. Nothing less than a comprehensive recorded catalog of his brain waves could prove otherwise.

The Forgotten Genius

On January 7, 1943, Nikola Tesla died in New York City at the age of 87. He was virtually penniless, living at the dilapidated Hotel New Yorker in a room that he shared with a flock of pigeons, which he considered his only friends.

The thriving industries he had built had long since turned their backs on him. The scientific community shunned him and his eccentric views. To the general public, he was either unknown or an object of ridicule, a lunatic whose ravings were fit only for sensational tabloids. The popular Max Fleischer "Superman" cartoons of the 1940s pitted the Man of Steel against the death rays and electromagnetic terrors of a scheming mad scientist, whose name was Tesla.

How could this have happened? Whatever his flaws, however far afield he may have strayed at times, Tesla surely deserved better than this. Modern society owes him just as much as the people of his time did, if not more, and yet we have forgotten him.

There are several schools of thought on the question of Tesla's fall into obscurity. The first, and probably the most irrefutable, is that Tesla failed to make the history books because he failed as a businessman. The most successful people aren't necessarily the most brilliant, but those who can play the game to reach the top. Tesla was a disciple of the pure sciences as opposed to applied science, with little facility at figuring out how to profit from his ideas. His business associates often did not act on behalf of his best interests, and Tesla himself made scores of bad financial decisions.

For example, in the wake of Tesla's successful implementation of AC, he stood to collect an enormous amount of wealth. He had signed a contract with Westinghouse which could conceivably have put him among the richest men in America. But when George Westinghouse told Tesla that the financial drain of the arrangement would put his company's future in jeopardy, Tesla ripped the contract to shreds, as a gesture of friendship. Had he held Westinghouse to the deal, or at least negotiated for a fraction of it, Tesla would have died in luxury, and may have preserved his notoriety much more fittingly.

Other analysts take the blame off Tesla's shoulders, and propose that big business and the U.S. government conspired to suppress the inventor's genius. At the top of the suspected conspirator list is Thomas Edison. Edison despised his former employee's success with AC, and it is known that he set out on a campaign to smear Tesla's name. He held demonstrations at which animals were lethally electrocuted with AC-powered devices, in a deceptive and inhumane effort to warn the public of the danger posed by Tesla and Westinghouse's "unsafe" new electrical system. Edison also sat on the War Department advisory board that rejected Tesla's proposals of the death ray and his radar-like device.

J. P. Morgan is also implicated in the anti-Tesla cover-up. Morgan counted on increasing his already monumental wealth by exploiting Tesla's ideas, until he learned that Tesla was considering the free distribution of energy - a terrifying idea to any self-respecting capitalist. He ended his funding of Tesla's experiments at once, and some think he used his considerable clout to ensure that no one else would bankroll Tesla's threatening schemes.

The government, which had always held Tesla at arm's length when he attempted to pitch a proposal, became suddenly fascinated with his work as soon as he died. The FBI ordered the Office of Alien Property to seize all of Tesla's papers and possessions. This confiscation was unequivocally illegal, since Tesla had been an American citizen since 1891.

The records of Tesla's work were judged to pose no threat to national security, and the FBI's file on Tesla was closed in 1943. It was reopened in 1957 in the wake of reports that the Russians were performing mysterious Tesla technology experiments. Many are convinced the Pentagon has followed suit with top-secret Tesla-based projects of its own, the most infamous being HAARP, the High-frequency Active Auroral Research Program. Reminiscent of Tesla's giant magnifying transmitter, only pointed in the opposite direction, the $30-million experiment is designed to pump enormous quantities of energy into the atmosphere over Alaska. The purposes of HAARP are unclear, although researchers probing the project have called it everything from a communications and surveillance network to a mass mind-control device.

A final theory is that Tesla ruined his reputation with his own outlandish inventions and claims. Some claim that Tesla went wrong as soon as he struck upon his quest for wireless energy. Others believe that he descended into insanity or senility when he began to speak of death rays and Martians. Tesla never accepted the work of Albert Einstein, which he criticized as being vague and incoherent. Given his adherence to these beliefs, many question how great a scientist Tesla could have been.

Strictly speaking, such arguments are probably correct. To the best of modern scientific knowledge, Tesla's free energy system simply would not work, there are no signals broadcast from Mars, and the theory of relativity is sound. But there are two things left to consider.

First, even if Tesla's later ideas were dead wrong, they by no means diminish the immense quantity of very right ideas that he contributed to our world. And second, it bears remembering that alternating current was also perceived as unrealistic Tesla gibberish for quite some time before its true brilliance was finally proven. There is the possibility, however remote, that Tesla's most bizarre concepts will be validated at some point in the future, when science finally catches up with him. Only time will tell.

For now, Tesla's true legacy is increasingly being recognized, bit by bit. The Supreme Court ruled shortly after his death that Tesla was the legal inventor of radio, not Guglielmo Marconi. Similarly, Tesla has been rightfully acknowledged as the inventor of the fluorescent bulb, the vacuum tube amplifier and the X-ray machine. History books are now starting to include these facts. Finding exposure in our current so-called "information age," in which technology is king and strange new ideas are tolerated more and more, Tesla is becoming something of a folk hero. This may run the risk of reducing Tesla and his work to an Internet fad, but any effort that keeps his name alive is worthwhile.

The final fate of Tesla's Wardenclyffe laboratory was strangely fraught with meaning. In 1917, it was consigned to demolition. Tesla's money for its upkeep had run dry, and its meager remaining contents were reportedly coveted by German spies. As a preemptive move, it was dynamited. But the proud steel tower of Wardenclyffe remained. The demolition crew blasted the site repeatedly, but the tower would not collapse. They had to return at a later date and dynamite it once more. It fell to the ground, but did not explode, nor did it shatter into pieces upon its thunderous impact.

OTIS T. CARR

Otis T. Carr with wooden mock-up of OTC-X1

Otis T. Carr – Carrying on the Tesla Flame

AFTER Nikola Tesla's death in 1943, it seemed as if there would be no one able to carry on with his legacy. At that time, Tesla was forgotten; his accomplishments marginalized by those who sought to steal or suppress the great man's inventions and theories. One man, however, was not afraid to try to continue on with Tesla's dreams. This man was Otis T. Carr.

Carr was born in 1904 in Elkins, West Virginia. He briefly attended the Ohio School of Commercial Art in Cleveland and later became a member of a group of artists in New York City. Carr claimed that he first met Tesla in 1925, while working as a hotel clerk in Manhattan. Nikola Tesla had a penchant for feeding pigeons in a nearby park, and Carr was asked to obtain a bag of unsalted peanuts so that Tesla could feed his beloved birds.

Even though Nikola Tesla was reclusive, the two men developed a friendship that lasted right up until the time of Tesla's death. Carr said that their friendship led to discussions about science and technological developments for new forms of energy production. Once, when the two men visited the Museum of Natural History in New York, Tesla told Carr to study the Cape York Meteorite and to learn a message from it. Carr reported he was able to obtain harmonic sounds from the iron meteorite using a hammer and he drew certain electromagnetic patterns from that.

After Tesla's death, Carr wrote a book titled, *Dimensions of Mystery: A Message for the Twentieth Century. Dimensions of Mystery* was a collection of poetry, allegorical stories, and a report on the discovery of free energy...no doubt inspired by his friendship with Tesla. Around 1955, Carr created OTC Enterprises with the purpose of developing inventions using Tesla technology.

By no stretch of the imagination could Otis T. Carr by considered a scientist, nor did he claim to be. What is likely is that Nikola Tesla shared with his young friend his ideas of utilizing new forms of energy to power a field propulsion generator. This type of "antigravity" propulsion had been conceived by Tesla years before, but technology at that time prevented him from going beyond laboratory experiments. With Tesla's notes in hand, Carr was certain that with the help of engineers who were not afraid to "think outside of the box," Tesla's dreams could at last become a reality.

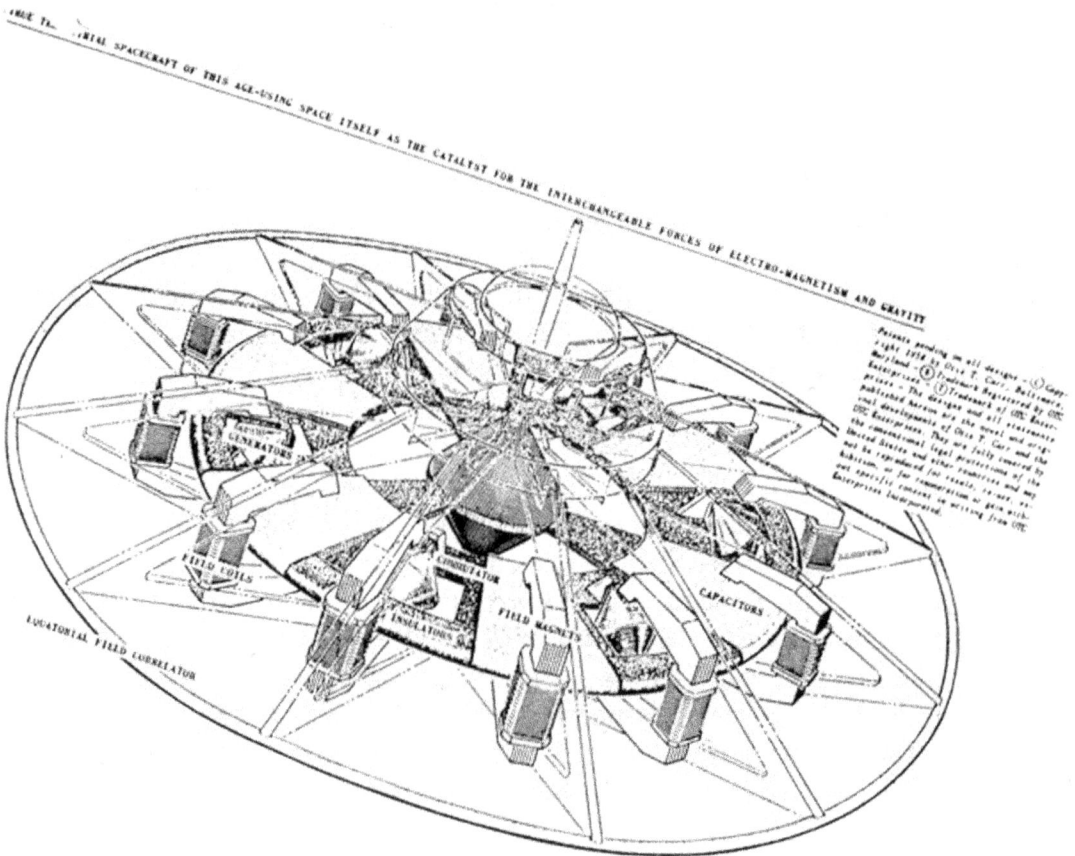

OTC-X1

FATE magazine - May 1958 - page 17

Gravity Machine?

The following summary was sent from a ship's onboard newspaper of October 30, 1957, after being copied from a *CW News* broadcast while at sea. It is unusual because no other report of this announcement reached us. It certainly is sensational - if true.

Baltimore, Md., October 29 - A group of inventors claimed Monday they have been able to utilize gravity in circular motion machines capable of powering everything from hearing aids to space cruisers.

Otis T. Carr, president of OTC Enterprises, Inc., detailed his claims in an interview and demonstration of a crude model of a circular motion machine which he said is the principle of a "free energy circular foil" space craft he can build, if someone puts up the money.

He said the machine can be adapted to devices of any size to produce continuous power absolutely free of dissipation.

Its immediate application, Carr said, would be in a spacecraft - which would be able to fly among the planets in controlled flight. It could land or take off as desired on the earth, the moon or any planet in the earth's solar system, he said.

Carr and his associates said their claims are based on the most simple practical applications of natural laws and discoveries in science and mathematics. They have no formal education in science or engineering.

He said the same "free energy" which causes the earth to rotate on its axis and orbit around the sun will turn a machine he described as two cones joined at their circular bases.

When the rotation of such a machine reaches a certain velocity relative to the earth's orbital velocity, Carr said, it will take off.

Carr said the core of his space ship would be a huge battery which would spin at the velocity of the external craft and which would be recharged, he said, by its motion. Carr declared such a battery, built to any size, could be designed to power the largest electric generating plant, operate an automobile, heat a house or power any conceivable machine or device.

The principle on which Carr said such circular motion machines would operate is that "any vehicle" accelerated to an axis rotation relative to its attractive inertial mass (the earth) immediately becomes activated by free space energy and acts as an independent force.

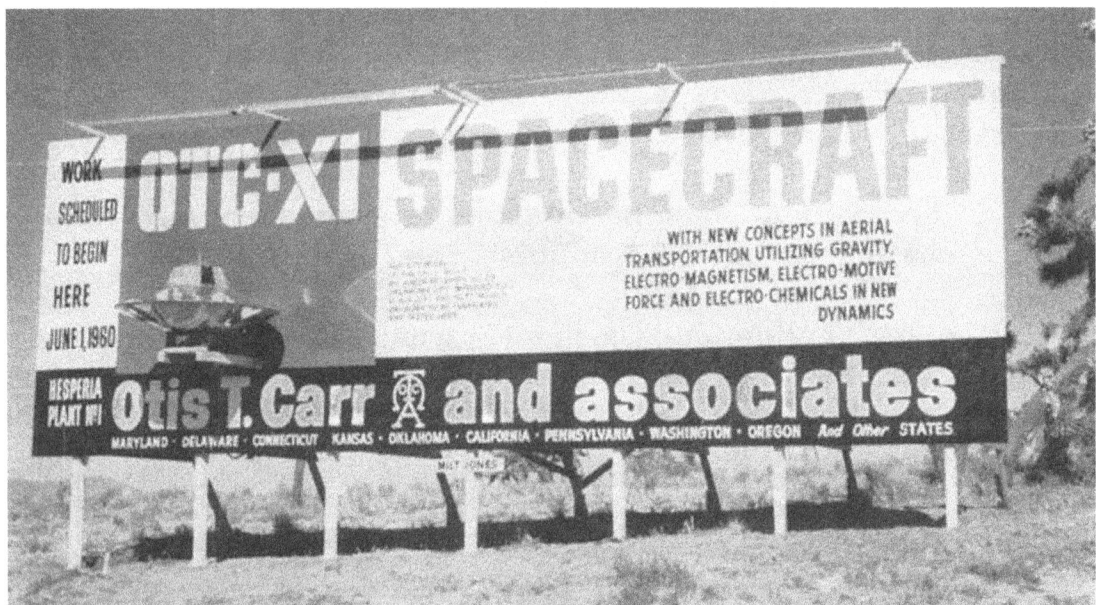

The Otis T. Carr Story
From *Return of the Dove* by Margaret Storm

USUALLY people look upon the training of a disciple as something extremely mystical and esoteric, something that takes place within a lamasery or secluded retreat, far from the haunts of men and pigeons. But in this instance... and it is certainly one of the most successful instances of discipleship on record... most of the training took place on the steps of the New York public library.

Day after day, in good weather and bad, young Carr carried peanuts to Tesla. And day after day, the elderly scientist and his young protégé strolled slowly along certain streets where flocks of pigeons were wont to gather in anticipation of the scattered nutmeats. The pilgrimage usually ended on the steps of the library on the west side, facing Bryant Park. There the two sat side by side, with Tesla luring the birds to eat out of his hand, while he explained to young Carr the fascinating details of their mysterious intelligence.

Tesla is said to have talked but little in those years, but fortunately young Carr was not inhibited by any knowledge of this fact. He asked the great genius so many questions and listened with such rapt eagerness to every syllable, that Tesla soon gave him a nickname... The sponge. This served as a little joke between two good friends, but actually the name was well chosen as Tesla realized when he selected it.

When the average disciple is in training, he gushes forth questions like a fountain in full play. It would seem to an observer that such an individual could not possibly absorb the answers, even if answers are forthcoming from a teacher. Usually they are not, for the wise teacher merely listens, and from time to time, when he can get a word, he offers certain explanations.

It was in November 1957...that same glad November, decked with a sparkle and a twinkle, and with long, tall nights stretching upward to the stars... when Otis T. Carr of Baltimore, Maryland, announced that free energy and space flight had been once again made available to the inhabitants of this planet.

Carr, a disciple of Tesla, has come up with two new inventions. One is an electrical accumulator and the other a gravity motor, both utilizing the power of the Sun and other forces of nature found in free abundance in the atmosphere. They are strictly free energy devices, which Carr claims may be used to power anything from a hearing aid to a spaceship.

Although they are machines, just as surely as the Tesla anti-war machine is a mechanical device, yet they follow the principles of nature so closely as to be almost organic in function. Like other New Age mechanisms, the Carr machines point the way to what may be expected from Ascended Master Saint Germain's scientific program for the Aquarian Age. The gap between organic and inorganic science is being closed rapidly, even in the minds of the laboratory experts who created the breach in the first place. The gap did not exist in actuality. It existed only in the minds of those who peered through very, very inadequate microscopes.

It was because of this delusion concerning the gap that science separated itself off from religion. The only religion that will bind one back to the Source, in the correct meaning of the word, is the science of man's evolution. The church that a man attends plays no part in his evolution, except perhaps to retard it. God is pure energy and He does not attend a church. He is also pure love, and He desires that His prodigal children return home to Him at the earliest possible moment. We can only go home to the Father's house when we have finished with our classroom work on this Earth.

The entire Aquarian Age program is, therefore, dependant upon having an abundance of leisure time for evolutionary study. We must give up that ancient device of earning our living by the sweat of our brow, get busy with our homework, and make our Ascension.

Master Saint Germain is well aware that machines are necessary to accomplish the Aquarian program for all people everywhere. The homespun way of life may be quaint and even colorful, but is it dreadfully inefficient. There are ten billion souls who must be process through this Earth training center during the next two thousand years. There will not be time for anyone to sit around doing hand-embroidery in order to pass away the hours.

Actually the New Age machinery, much of it invented by Saint Germain Himself, is ready and waiting. But humanity is not ready to accept it. Therefore, in the interim period it is necessary for men like Carr and Matthews to invent machines which will carry the world peacefully through the transition period. Further, such inventions serve to anchor the New Age energies in physical matter, raising its vibrations and lifting karma, and that is a very important factor from the Hierarchical point of view. Adepts are not permitted to just hand out inventions to the human race, however desirable those inventions may be.

That is why men like Tesla, Matthews, and Carr, must serve as outposts of consciousness. They have human free will and can put forward inventions without imposing on the free will of others. It is up to humanity to accept or reject inventions which are offered in the open competitive market.

Carr has realized this fully, and has organized a solid business corporation under the normal conventions of the American free enterprise system. This is the system which prevails today, for good or for evil, and in order not to interfere with man's free will Carr has arranged his enterprise to fit into the established way of life.

It may not be tomorrow's way of life, but it exists today and we must accept it in good grace until change is indicated. Adjustments must proceed in an orderly manner, for it is the desire of the Hierarchy and the space people that the transition from the old age to the new be made without fear or panic, stress or strain. There is no need to talk of impending cataclysms, for with the straightening of the Earth's axis in 1958, the greatest period of danger is over.

It was on a summer day in 1925 that Otis T. Carr was busy with his new duties as a package clerk in a large mid-town hotel in New York. He had just arrived in the city to study art, and he found employment in order to cover his tuition. First, he had felt impelled to come to New York. Upon arrival, he had felt impelled to apply for a job in a particular hotel. He was put to work at once and was just getting acquainted with his surroundings when Nikola Tesla wound his prophetic way through the subterranean passages of the lower basement and approached the new package clerk.

"When you finish your duties here." said Tesla with grave dignity, "go out and buy four pounds of unsalted peanuts and bring them to my suite," He handed the lad from Elkins, West Virginia, sufficient money to cover the purchase, plus a generous gratuity. The gratuity was part of the Tesla legend; to him the laborer was very, very worthy of his hire.

Otis was not surprised at the nature of the request because, as he had often been told, in New York one could expect anything to happen. It was not in the least like Elkins. The package clerk carried out the order and delivered the peanuts to Tesla. Meanwhile he had made a few inquiries among the other clerks, and he found that Tesla was a great scientist who fed peanuts to pigeons. He even took care of the sick and injured pigeons and kept many of them in baskets upstairs in his suite.

Upon making the delivery, young Carr was invited by Tesla to come in for a chat. This was the beginning of one of the most unusual and most fascinating stories of discipleship that has yet come to light in modern times.

Esoteric training is based on certain scriptural phrases: Before you have asked, I have answered. Ask and you shall receive. Knock and it shall be opened unto you. Seek and you shall find. I am the Way, the Truth and the Light.

It is this attitude of seeking, questioning, asking, constant wonderment, that is the hallmark of the disciple. Direct answers from a teacher are not only unnecessary, but often confusing. It is absolutely necessary for the disciple to ask, for that is the spiritual Law. The Presence will do the answering when and if necessary. The Presence does not pour useless knowledge into the brain of a student. Only school teachers do that sort of thing. A disciple may ask a question and wait twenty-five or fifty years for an answer, but when the answer comes, as it surely will, it will flash into the mind at the exact moment that it is needed.

Therefore, when Tesla teasingly named young Carr "The Sponge," he indicated that he knew Carr was storing up knowledge that he could draw upon at any time in the future when he truly needed it. Assuredly, he did not need to understand the workings of the universe in order to sit on the steps of the library with Tesla and toss peanuts to pigeons.

Tesla's correct attitude was proved again and again during the thirty years that followed the three-year period of Carr's training. Carr never saw Tesla again or had further contact with him after the third year. During the thirty subsequent years, Carr spent hours daily in his own little workshop, performing the thousands of experiments that led to final success with the gravity motor and electric propulsion system. There in the workshop he found that he could, at any time, dip into the reservoir of his photographic memory, and bring forth in total recall every needed thought concerning sine wave or coil winding or other Tesla applications and innovations.

Carr had no formal engineering training, nor had he any knowledge of esotericism before meeting Tesla. However, he was so inspired by the superman that he later steeped himself in philosophies of the east and the west, and ranged far and wide in his reading and studying, covering a vast field of knowledge. Like the martyred Bruno, Carr has come to be known as the academician without academy.

As he read and studied over the years, he always followed Tesla's example by going straight to the heart and brain of nature for his knowledge. He quickly discovered how to sort the absolutes from the mountains of dialectic chaff in the world's accumulated words and works. He never wasted precious time repeating what was proved.

As a result of his great perceptive guidance, it is estimated that Carr has advanced scientific achievement at least a century by concrete application of his free energy discoveries. Like Tesla, he harbors no secrets about his inventions. He is more than happy to discuss them with anyone who will listen. Also, like Tesla, he has been unable thus far to sell them or even give them away. But that situation will change rapidly for both Carr and Tesla... probably in a matter of weeks now... as Saint Germain's new Aquarian program gets into full swing.

Carr, philosophically at least, is already allied with Ascended Master Saint Germain, inasmuch as Saint Germain share in the development of the business as it unfolds. Aside from the fact that he is definitely opposed to any monopolistic practices, so common in big business, his corporate structure is not unlike that of other successful world producers.

The basic design for all his business stationary, brochures, booklets, and so forth, is not only interesting and original, but extremely symbolic. His initials, OTC, are arranged so as to form the sign of Omega. Surmounting this is the White Dove... Tesla's Dove... in full, graceful flight. Below is the motto which reads: Peace and plenty through the application of free energy to supply all things to all people.

Carr has already met the same resistance from the forces of darkness that plagued Tesla, and, as usual, it comes through money channels and threats of economic boycott... this time in relation to newspaper advertising. In launching an announcement of his inventions Carr had a full-page advertisement prepared for insertion in a leading daily paper of Baltimore. The advertisement was paid for and accepted by the paper. Shortly thereafter it was cancelled by the newspaper and the money refunded. The newspaper had to cancel the advertising at the request of one of their big money-spenders who had metered power, not free energy, for sale to the public. Therefore, the people of Baltimore and vicinity were not even privileged to know that one of their own citizens had invented free energy devices capable of powering everything from a hearing aid to a spaceship.

While the governments still deny the existence of flying saucers, and daily newspapers refuse to give outstanding news to their readers in the form of a paid advertisement, the uninformed public remains uninformed. They do not even know that the problem of space flight has been solved.

Scientists have said that no individual in an unascended body can make a trip into outer space. If governments do not believe in the existence of flying saucers from outer Space, then they cannot accept the fact that the space people have a station on the Moon. Why, then, do they hesitate to use a Carr spaceship to go to the Moon, and find out for themselves what is up there?

It seems obvious that they do know there is a space station on the Moon. Undoubtedly, the space people have told them that they will not be permitted to land, and they know the space people mean business. In the meantime they can keep on playing with their rocket toys in order to fool the taxpayer, and give the impression that he is getting something big and grand for his money.

Carr is not planning to have a large spaceship ready for flight for at least a year. It is quite possible that he could make a trip to the Moon and be permitted to land there. Inasmuch as he would be testing his own ship, the trip would have no military significance, and he is entirely in accord with the program set up by the space people. Also, by the time he has a ship of sufficient size ready for a voyage into outer space, it might be possible for him to make that trip too, especially if one or more space persons would agree to accompany him. But these conjectures are entirely unique and apply only to Carr.

What he can or cannot accomplish has nothing to do with the attitude of governments which first refuse to admit the possibility of spaceships from other planets and then refuse to try out a local model. Supposing it is not entirely successful on the trial run? It certainly could not be less successful than many of the rockets and satellites which the government is attempting to launch at the expense of the taxpayers.

Why the secrecy? Why are people not being told that an American citizen is building a spaceship on this planet? They are not even told that it is now possible to power everything with free energy drawn from the atmosphere; that we need no longer be enslaved by petroleum, coal and old forms of fuel.

This is news of world importance, yet so strict is the gangster censorship imposed by the Silence Group, that newspapers founded for the purpose of giving news to the public dare not carry out their function, for to do so would mean running the risk of ruinous economic sanctions. However, Carr and his associates displayed no resentment over the refusal of the daily newspaper to carry the advertising. Instead, they placed page ads in small suburban weeklies which were overjoyed to have the sudden business windfall.

The result was not only amazing, but proved conclusively that the public wanted to be informed about Carr's inventions. From far and wide, letters of inquiry began to pour in. Hundreds of extra copies of the newspapers were requested to be sent to relatives and friends in distant states and countries. Request for literature on the Carr machines reached huge proportions, and continued to soar day after day. Scores of people sent in small amounts of money... from a dollar to five dollars... as a down payment on stock that was not even offered for sale. Visitors began to arrive with requests for information on everything from vast power plants to spaceships.

Meanwhile Carr had offered to build and deliver space ships to governments wishing to send expeditions to the Moon or elsewhere, but these offers were declined in favor of much more expensive rocket and missile programs.

This is a most interesting and intriguing development. The space people have stated that they will not permit military or tourist landings on the Moon. The Hierarchy has had His last embodiment as Francis Bacon at which time He wrote plays and sonnets under the pseudonym of William Shakespeare. Otis Carr has rooted his entire development in a total acceptance of Shakespeare's poetic dictum:

"There's a divinity that shapes our ends, Rough-hew them how we will."

Carr is a man who is characterized by an attitude of constant gratefulness. He is not only grateful to God and to Tesla, but his gratitude extends back to Archimedes and forward to Einstein, for he feels that the application of certain scientific principles down through the ages by countless discoverers and scientists, all contributed to his own inventions. This attitude is especially apparent in Carr's speech and writings. He stubbornly sticks to the plural form, we, in his narration of accomplishment.

When questioned about this he spoke of the total principles proved by the great men of history, and how each proof had entered into his final concept of the gravity motor and electrical accumulator. He acknowledges Archimedes' lever, Copernicus' constants, Galileo's acceleration, Newton's motions, Faradat's coil, Bacon' prerogatives, Edison's thermionics, Einstein's relativity, Franklin's static, Galvini's electrolysis, and Tesla's understanding of outer space; and the works of craftsmen like Fulton, Ford, and the Wright brothers, whose "follies, foibles, and infernal-machines' would never, it was said, perform the 'fantasies' that are now commonplace.

Like Tesla, Carr desires that his inventions serve all humanity, not a privileged few. It is his wish that millions of individuals from all nations will have an opportunity to lead lives free of poverty and hunger. Technology can turn Earth into a utopia as long as it is not used by the privileged for war and death. Furthermore, a rocket leads but to destruction. A spaceship leads to the freedom of the cosmic lightways and opens a vast new universe to the wonderment of man.

Since Carr's free energy devices are designed to power anything from a hearing aid to a spaceship, it is clear why his advertising is refused by daily newspapers, and why the government refuses to even try a Carr spaceship on the national budget... just for size, at least. Carr's free energy motors will power automobiles, for one thing; a development which would do away with the need for gasoline and as an added advantage do away with smelly exhaust fumes.

For years, geologists and scientists have been bemoaning the fact that our natural fuels such as petroleum will soon be exhausted. They have painted grim word pictures of a shivering, stranded populace, hovering over a meager fire of sticks and twigs, and just about to perish for lack of fuel. Yet when Otis T. Carr announces free energy motors the newspapers hasten to keep the whole thing hush-hush lest the people find out that they will not have to shiver after all.

There is still another reason why the Silence Group, operating through black disciples in the military and commercial business arenas, has decreed that Carr's inventions should be played down. Carr is obviously working on behalf of the Forces of Light and he is probably the first man in history who has had the courage to incorporate that theme in his paid newspaper advertising.

He is irrevocably against mistreatment of the atom, for well he knows that an atom is God's handiwork, and a tiny pulsing life. In the advertisement, he states that his machines are natural machines; that they produce unlimited energy without fission, without fusion, and without violence of any kind. They do not smash the atom. They do not split the atom. They do not blast the atom.

He reminds his readers that his machines are profoundly simple devices that collect and direct the free and boundless energies of the Sun "in the same way the Sun's energies cause the Earth to spin and the rivers to flow, the bread to rise and the plants to grow, and the great ocean tides to rise and fall." He states that the accumulator uses the Sun's force of electro-magnetism by means of natural reproductive chemistry, and that the motor is powered entirely by the Sun's immutable pressure energy known as gravity.

He sums up not only his method but his philosophy as follows:

All energy is atomic
The light from the Sun
The pull of gravity
The fission of uranium
The fusion of hydrogen
All that moves

Or grows, or glows
Everywhere on Earth
And throughout the Universe.
It is all atomic energy.

Its utronic presence is everywhere,
Being even Nature itself.

And held in plain view for all
The time we know, it has yet
Remained Nature's closest secret.
So, how to borrow of this energy
From Nature, has been quite
A problem.

When you fight Nature
Nature always fights back.

If we try to share Nature's energy
By injuring Nature, we will only
Injure ourselves accordingly.

Try to change the weather in one
Place and you get storms, or floods,
Or drought in another.

Crack or split the atom and you
Get frightful devastation or
Poisonous radiation.

And while you may blast a dog or
A man away into Space, you will
Never safely blast him back again.

We know the laws of Nature do not
Change, so why waste the effort
And take the terrible risks?

There is only one right way.
The right way is the peaceful way.
And we have found the way!

Carr's architectural plans for a Space Research Institute to be located at Space, Maryland, have been drawn up, and preliminary construction activities are under way on a beautiful plot of land of about seventy acres, outside Baltimore. The new post office will be called Space.

Space Research Institute is expected to become the world center for activities connected with spaceships, interplanetary travel, interplanetary communication, and a better way of life through the utilization of natural solar energy devices. The group of buildings incorporate new design motifs which should make them outstanding in architectural beauty.

The plans call for a huge, domed auditorium. The interior of the dome will be decorated by Salvador Dali, who is currently preparing a huge mural masterpiece to be enshrined there. The subject is the prophetic story of Ezekiel's vision, approached from the space-time cosmogony. A total space concept is portrayed by four guardian cherubim. And over all hovers a portrait of the white Dove of Shamballa... Tesla's Earth companion.

Although Space Research Institute will serve as headquarters for the Otis T. Carr enterprises, he does not plan to mass-manufacture any of his devices. The institute, as its name implies, is strictly for research. There the group will design prototypes of machines which will then be turned over to other manufacturers to be produced in quantity. Mr. Carr has behind him the long history of Tesla's frustrated attempts to make the world a more comfortable place in which to live, and to give humanity countless hours of leisure time for study and evolutionary advancement. Therefore, his primary interest is not in becoming a manufacturer himself, but in the opportunity of all industry, the world over, to share in the ownership and distribution of products patterned after the basic prototypes.

Since Carr is a disciple of Tesla, and since Tesla refused to participate in the conniving, competitive commercial manipulations of his day, business men everywhere are eager to know how Carr, faced with problems almost identical to those of Tesla, plans to surmount the many obstacles which are certain to be placed in his way by the forces of darkness. The answer seems to be contained within the unilitarian functions of the inventions themselves. Once the public knows that the devices will provide a better way of life, it is up to the public to demand that the inventions be made available.

The OTC circular-foil spacecraft looks and operates like a flying saucer. The first experimental models will be anywhere from forty to a hundred feet in diameter, and will cost millions of dollars, as do first prototypes of any aircraft. However, one small model, ten feet in diameter will be constructed for special tests purposes in actual usage.

Unlike conventional aircraft, the large space vehicles will soon be brought down to family size of about ten feet in diameter. They can be built to sell for less than the cost of a modern automobile, and are designed to take a family across town, across the nation, or around the world in absolute comfort and safety, and in a fraction of the time ever before possible. Carr expects to be ready during 1959 to start licensing manufacturers all over the world to mass-produce the OTC space vehicles in many sizes and styles for every transportation need.

It is Mr. Carr's sincere opinion that the introduction, manufacture, and use of the free energy devices will bring more prosperity to more people in the United States and around the globe, than any single invention in the entire history of the world. He realizes that most of the world's problems today have their roots in hunger for more energy than is available.

"States and nations are already fighting over what is left of ordinary fuels and the available supplies of water to make electricity and irrigate the land," states Mr. Carr. "We have had many recent examples of our delicate balance of supply and demand, even in this great country. We've seen the rationing of gasoline and oil. We've seen the lights go dim in the Pacific Northwest.

"We've seen vast millions of burning desert acres barren only for lack of a little irrigation. And now even the oil men are beginning to squeeze the last drop out of every ton of shale.

"The power hunger is the same the world over, only it is more intense now. The most shocking recent example was the willingness of Egypt to close the Suez Canal and fight the world for a few kilowatts of electricity.

"Free energy devices can change all this in a remarkably short space of time. Enough electric power and energy in the right places, and we will have undreamed of markets for every other kind of goods and materials and appliances our factories and shops can turn out.

"And so goes the simple formula: Give the world enough electrical energy and you raise the world's standard of living. Raise the world's standard of living, and you raise the world's economy.

"The best way to get the total concept of what free energy means to the world today, is to suppose that the wheel were just now being discovered.

Then visualize the free energy motor putting the wheel into the air, into an entirely new dimension. Industry must realize that these devices will provide power for automobiles, trains, great ocean liners, and spaceships, as well as for such things as hearing aids, portable television sets, refrigerators, and will even furnish power, light, and heat for large cities or communities.

"Our free energy devices will do all these things by perpetual space-forces of magnetism, gravity, and electro-magnetism...and these forces alone; forces which are free and available everywhere on the face of the Earth and throughout the universe."

While the world is still groveling under the ancient edict that called for earning one's bread by the sweat of one's brow, the question of how free energy devices will affect employment is a paramount one. But Mr. Carr feels that his inventions and discoveries truly represent the inception of a basic new industry, which for sheer size and scope might be properly compared with the steel, automobile and aircraft industries combined. He believes that pioneering in a free energy will automatically introduce a new concept of employment practices and employee relationships.

Although the space people themselves have had no contact with Otis T. Carr and have had no direct hand in his work, it is safe to assume that they have been watching it carefully. In addition, Tesla and the dove have assuredly directed it from the scientific department of Shamballa, making certain that it will fit into the Divine Plan at exactly the right moment. This, then, is the right moment.

The grave danger that might have turned the entire enterprise into a gargantuan war machine is now over, for with the straightening of the Earth's axis completed, the Hierarchy and the space people will be able to neutralize major war efforts. There may be sporadic minor clashes, but even these may now be avoided. Lord Michael, Prince of the Archangels, has had such tremendous success in his house-cleaning efforts, that the final physical plane adjustments are not likely to be too formidable.

It was that keen observer of Nature, now the Ascended Master Saint Germain, who, in a former embodiment as Francis Bacon, set the stage for the new civilization which He is building today. His basic plan for mankind was revealed in a simple prefatory remark in Novum Organum: "If man would conquer Nature, man must join with Nature."

Francis Bacon is an outstanding example of a man who successfully refused, through 70,000 years as a civilization-builder, to fight against Nature. As a result of this simple cooperative method, the floodgates of wisdom remained open to him. This resolute leader of humanity could look back down the corridors of the centuries with full continuity of consciousness, and review the events which had carried the whole human race to the threshold of the Aquarian Age.

Transmutation is the keynote of the Aquarian program for mankind. Any effort which man now makes to join Nature, helps to lift some of the heavy karma he has created by fighting Nature in the past.

Otis. T. Carr has recognized the true responsive Nature of the atom when it is treated as an Intelligence. "Essentially, what we have done is collect, arrange, adapt and orchestrate some of Nature's compositions into harmonious assemblage," he explains. "They are fashioned out of God's creation. They are instruments of peace. Their music is for all the worlds of man."

We have come very, very far into the Light since the dark, uncertain days of 1955, when it seemed that the worst cataclysmic prophecies of Armageddon were about to be fulfilled. As Arthur H. Matthews so joyfully states: "Be of good courage, for we have God with us. And we have the spirit of Tesla with us."

Yes, indeed we have! All this, and the White dove, too. We seem to hear the gentle rustle of white wings around us: we seem to hear the gentle voice of Nikola enfolding us; comforting us, assuring us that he still walks beside the one who was obedient to his command: Go forth! Explore Space! There in the limitless azure skies is your rendezvous with Destiny.

Otis T. Carr on the Long John Nebel Show

THE public first heard about Otis T. Carr in 1957 on the wildly popular late-night radio program, *The Long John Nebel Show*, broadcast from WOR in New York. Carr announced that OTC Enterprises would manufacture a flight capable circular foil spacecraft, which would be offered for sale at twenty million dollars. He explained that his confidence and knowledge for building such a machine resulted from actually seeing three electrified saucers and through his consultations with the eminent scientist, Nikola Tesla.

Even though Nebel doubted Carr's claims, he remained a popular guest on the show and made a number of appearances. He also spoke to business groups and school audiences and went on a cross-country lecture tour to UFO audiences. He would explain how his invention, the Utron Accumulator would generate free energy, due in part to the geometry of joining two cones to form a square.

Thanks to the website Keelynet.com, Mike Hughes of Anaheim, California, and Jerry Decker, we have the transcript of one of Carr's appearances on the *Long John Nebel Show*. The conversation on this 1957 show was between Long John Nebel, Otis T. Carr and Norman Colton.

L.J. - According to the schedule here the delivered price payable in full on delivery, with no prior commitments required, and including all poolings, and other overhead is 20 million dollars. Additional identical units are on the same schedule for 4 million dollars each. That's a lot of money! My name is Long John and we call this 'the Party Line.'

I imagine you wonder what I'm talking about for 20 million dollars. Well, I've had a few sponsors and we've sold a few things, but I don't have O.T.C. Enterprises Inc. of Baltimore, Maryland as sponsor but they do have something to sell. Mainly, a circular foil spacecraft that is available for 20 million dollars. We have talked about flying saucers on the program many times. But tonight it appears to me we have two very solid citizens who represent O.T.C. Enterprises and according to all of the brochures, all of the booklets, everything we have in front of us and believe me we have a stack of things in front of us, including miniature working models, and with all of this material. I'm led to believe these men and believe that there is something to flying saucers.

And the men that I'm referring to are Otis. T. Carr, President and Norman Evans Colton, Director of Sales Engineering. These gentlemen are associated with O.T.C. Enterprises, and we'll be talking with them tonight about the possibility of making a craft that can go to Venus, that can go to the moon, that can go to Mars, that costs 20 million dollars. And after we have the first one the rest of them won't cost too much, about 4 million dollars each. We have with us this morning Ben I. and Mel Saloney. They will be doing a lot of talking with a lot of people and I hope that you might call some of your friends and neighbors and tell them that if they are interested in flying saucers, this is one night that they should be with us.

Mr. Carr, some time ago one of our listeners sent me a brochure that was published by O.T.C. Enterprises. It's a very beautiful brochure; it's certainly a very inspiring one, and when I read this offer about a spacecraft that would be made available for 20 million dollars, I nearly flipped and I mentioned it on the air, and evidently somebody contacted your Director of Sales Engineering, Mr. Colton and he contacted us and that's why you're here this morning.

Before we talk about the particular space craft that you intend to manufacture, I would like to ask you a couple of questions. One; Do you believe in the possibility of flying saucers coming to this planet, the planet Earth, from other planets?

O.T.C. - We believe that there are unidentified electrified objects in the air. We have seen three on three separate occasions.

L.J. - Do you say you've seen three Mr. Carr? Did you see them in the air? Were they hovering above a particular location?

O.T.C. - In the air, they were going at great velocity and they were definitely electrified because we have been working on the same principle for many years and we recognize what we saw.

L.J. - Well when you say electrified, what other type, if we may use the word saucers this morning because many of our listeners understand that, what other type of saucers could there be other than electrified, could there be gas driven or something Sir?

O.T.C. - There could be if we followed principles now known within our atmosphere. There are many manners in which a circular craft could be used, such as the helo principal and jets on the area close to the foil, the leading edge. But in the incidents of the three different ones which we saw in 1951 and 1952 they were definitely electrical and they were very close to what we had already designed.

L.J. - Did you say the 'Helo' system?

O.T.C. - That's right. Well any system of circular rotation that can use a motive power such as jet propulsion would make an airborne craft.

L.J. - In what way is your invention different from the unidentified flying objects which you have seen?

O.T.C. - We do not know, naturally not having been able to examine the objects we saw due to the great velocity, we can't say with certainty that they are similar to ours, but the principle we feel is the same. Our design utilizes gravity, electro-magnetism, and electromotive force and a relative field to get its functional operation.

L.J. - I haven't understood a single word of your last sentence. Without getting at all technical could you sort of make it a little bit easier?

O.T.C. - We use this statement that we use an electrified sender. It's a central power core. Now this is what we call an 'accumulator.' In a vernacular sense, it is a factory. It is a storage cell, an accumulation of storage cells which provide an electromotive force in the same manner that any known battery produces an electromotive force.

L.J. - Is that what you are holding in your hand there?

O.T.C. - That's right.

L.J. - Can you describe it?

O.T.C. - This is a dimensional object. It was designed with the dimensions of space itself. We say it is truly the geometric form of space, because it is completely round and completely square. Now in this surface they are all round but when we show it this way the surfaces are square. It has been proven in scientific laboratories that the very smallest unit of mass matter ever photographed in the electron microscope are square in shape. This has only been found out in the last couple of months. We have known it for years and have applied this principle into an electrified system, which is the power core of our space vehicle. Now what makes this different and unique and novel from a battery is the fact that this is a piece of moving machinery that rotates. Our average storage battery is an inanimate object set in an inertial spot and then the electromotive force is conducted by wires from this battery to animate some object.

L.J. - Let me interrupt a moment, I'll try to describe it further. Well it looks like two ice cream cones put together at the wide ends, but the angle is a lot wider than that of the ice cream cones. There are a series of ridges that look like gears would fit in. Is that correct?

O.T.C. - No, those are in a sense 'turbines principles'. They are 'reactive channels'. And where there is atmosphere a flow of air there aids rotation.

L.J. - Well then, is this one of the components of the drive, this is the battery?

O.T.C. - This is the central power core.

L.J. - This generates electricity?

O.T.C. - This is right. This is a storage cell for electrical energy. In operation it generates electricity at the same time it puts out electromotive force. This is the central power system for our space craft.

L.J. - I can tell this, that it opened up and it appears to be hollowed out on the inside, much, I would say....well it's circular, the inside, when the two parts are put one on top of the other and they fit into place, the cavity inside is circular.

O.T.C. - It is a sphere, yes. And each unit is a hemisphere. We call the center of this, this large dimension the equator and of course it contracts and expands to a point on each side. It's the union of two conical sections, that is what it is. Two right angle sections, and we say it is the dimensions of space and we have shown how this comes about.

L.J. - This is Tuesday morning October 29th, 1957....Here is a paragraph that you sent copies of your brochure outlining your system of propulsion that you have developed to President Eisenhower and the Cabinet and the Atomic Energy Commission. Have you received an answer from them?

O.T.C. - There was recognition of receiving the material.

L.J. - Beyond that did they give any value judgment on what you had to contribute?

O.T.C. - No, we have not received any value judgment.

L.J. - Don't you think that is a little odd?

O.T.C. - Yes, I do.

L.J. - Is there any way that you can explain it?

O.T.C. - I have my own ideas about this. Of course no way to substantiate such ideas. To give my own personal opinion, we have a truly safe vehicle which is not expendable, it does not burn up its energy in a few seconds, it carries the energy with it, it can leave the earth's atmosphere and return man, it also can be used within the atmosphere. It can make a trip as easily as other aerial transportation systems from here to Baltimore or from here to the moon. Now it is inexpensive, it certainly doesn't cost as much as the systems of the expanding rocket. The fueling is much less expensive and whether or not our offer is entering into an economic picture that is not feasible at this time, we don't know. This is one of our opinions.

Ben - Mr. Carr. I've been glancing at the literature that you provided us with. I've been going over it and there is a mathematical formula that crops up here that intrigues me, minus zero divided by plus zero equals zero. The first time I ever saw a minus zero is in a mathematical equation in the work of Einstein. I wonder if you can tell me more about it and how you stumbled upon this idea.

O.T.C. - The equation is brought about by the shape of our Utron electrical accumulator, this is the name given to our central power system. In our operation of working models and in checking out experiments, we had to find the formula that fit the reason for the action and reaction we were getting. So in exploring nature and studying the great inspirational work of Dr. Einstein on relativity, we came upon this formula of linear correlation. And when we study linear correlation in geometric form, we have to have a starting point and this is the point. And from there it expands through the cross and through the circle. And the mathematics, the only way we can express it, is in the symbolism of zero X (or 0x) and this formula brings us to that. We claim that this is the true unified field theory in physical practice.

Ben - The thing I wonder about....is how you were led to the concept of a minus 0.

O.T.C. - In a further study of Dr. Einstein's great inspirational work and we corresponded with him and we had the great good fortune of being advised by him at one time, we learned that all measurements of time and space had to be considered in relationship to the observer and therefore there never was a fixed equation, due to the observer being an attempt, as I understand it, the observer himself being somewhat the minus factor and therefore you can't have any fixed quantity of any number. Now in physical form, this is something else again. We worked for a considerable time with and had many conferences with the great Nikola Tesla and his evaluation of the sine wave and electrical principles and the true value of alternating current and hydro-electric systems were developed by the great genius of this man. Further inspirations came to us and finally from this knowledge and continuing to seek we found this formula.

Ben - Did you find this formula, Mr. Carr?

O.T.C. - I found it with the assistance of Mr. Colton in the evaluation. Mr. Colton researches very heavily in all the work that I do and we collaborate very closely. Also Mr. Shea collaborates with me in research.

L.J. - Mr. Carr, when was O.T.C. incorporated?

O.T.C. - ...1955.

L.J. - And how long prior to the year 1955 were you associated with Mr. Shea and Mr. Colton?

O.T.C. - Not before that, they have come with me since then.

L.J. - Were you interested in this before 1955?

O.T.C. - We started, I use the editorial 'we', this development in 1937. Our investigations began in 1937. We were actively making models in 1938. In 1942 we had come up with the basic principles.

L.J. - In other words, 18 years prior to this year you had in your mind that possibly some type of craft could be developed that you could go into space with? Is that right?

O.T.C. - This is true.

L.J. - Do you hope with this craft, if you are able to manufacture it, that you can go to other planets with it?

O.T.C. - Escaping from the immediate gravity pull of the earth plus the heavy atmosphere of the earth enables us, just as our satellites are doing now, to join a universal free energy system. They have a velocity now of 18,000 miles per hour, more or less, without any expenditure of energy whatsoever. Now any energy attached to this would immediately throw them into a higher velocity orbit which would expand them further into space...This is extremely easy to do. We feel that our craft will gradually escape and possibly escape the atmosphere of the earth and then we can handle velocities almost unimaginable in reaching other gravity systems and the moon should not be more than five hours away.

L.J. - Five hours away from Baltimore, Maryland.

O.T.C. - That's right.

L.J. - How many people can you have in this craft?

O.T.C. - The one we have on the design board which is 45 feet in diameter, the cabin would accommodate three to be comfortable.

L.J. - And with type of equipment will you have on board of this craft?

O.T.C. - On this craft, insofar as the individuals are concerned, can travel the same as in a pressurized airliner. We don't have the problem of a heat shield.

L.J. - What about high velocity?

O.T.C. - We don't have a problem of thermal barriers because the electro-magnetic system sets up a protective shield in our craft which enables us to overcome this barrier without any discomfort to the occupants inside the craft. And we can very slowly rise, and once we are outside the atmosphere, we can accelerate to tremendous velocities up to the speed of light itself.

L.J. - I am greatly interested though in the method of landing this craft if you were able to get to the moon. Let's forget the moon a minute, if you get the craft up from this planet from the airport to Baltimore, how would it land sir?

O.T.C. - Back in Baltimore?

L.J. - Yes.

O.T.C. - Very simply, we can fly at a very slow velocity of 100/ft. per minute or less and we can sit down as gently as a feather because part of the operation of our craft has joined universal systems. This is a relative velocity of the attractive inertial mass, it becomes weightless as regards this inertial attraction. Individually, it is not weightless, it has the same weight as before, but when it reaches the relative location it becomes an independent system just as a planet is an independent system.

L.J. - Is there any gravitational pull at this point sir?

O.T.C. - None whatsoever.

L.J. - What happens to the occupants of the space craft?

O.T.C. - They are perfectly comfortable.

L.J. - I mean are their heads on the ceiling?

O.T.C. - Not at all. They will have the same feeling of pressure or weight that they have right now because we will maintain as near as possible the atmospheric pressure of the earth at sea level inside the craft.

L.J. - This is rather technical for me, Mr. Carr, so please accept my apologies for being rather stupid and ignorant in my line of questioning. I am under the impression that the only reason I'm able to sit in this chair, is because of gravitational pull.

O.T.C. - We have this at around 14 pounds per square inch within our atmosphere. We have been able to be sealed off away from such a condition and thus artificially with atmospheric pressure the pressure in the cabin is maintained. We have it very well in submarines. The same may be used in our craft.

L.J. - In other words, under sea, where a submarine may be, there is no gravitational pull, is that what you're saying?

O.T.C. - There is a gravitational pull at all times but we're speaking about the atmosphere of the particular occupants inside a sealed unit.

L.J. - Is that necessary to keep occupants in the position they desire.

O.T.C. - Absolutely, because in a vacuum they are at the mercy of any velocity.

L.J. - What would happen, sir, if there was some kind of instrument that you could turn on and eliminate the gravitation pull that was in this room?

O.T.C. - You would in a sense become very buoyant and this is not in itself a novelty but it certainly does not have any disastrous effects on humanity.

L.J. - Would I remain in this position?

O.T.C. - You could, but any movement could move you out of it.

L.J. - Would objects, the mike, remain in position?

O.T.C. - Until they were brought into any other movement. Any movement would make them buoyant themselves.

L.J. - I have a lead pencil, if I hold it in the air and release my fingers, it would fall because of gravitational pull.

O.T.C. - This is true.

L.J. - If we had this other condition which you so aptly described a moment ago, if I released my fingers would the pencil remain in midair?

O.T.C. - This is true, it would stay there.

L.J. - I believe what you are saying is that you'd be creating an artificial gravitational field within the body of the space craft and yet there would not be any gravity on the outside?

O.T.C. - Exactly correct.

L.J. - And this is done by the battery which I attempted to describe, spinning around and producing its own gravitational influence?

O.T.C. - Yes, this is the beginning of an answer to your question - we have capacitor plates and electro-magnets as a part of this system. Now this is counter-rotating, the electro-magnets rotate in one direction and the accumulator, the batteries rotate in another. The capacitor plates rotate in conjunction with the battery so that we have a clockwise and counter clockwise rotation. Now the third system is the cabin that maintains the crew. This does not rotate, it is fixed due to the fact the two bodies are rotating clockwise and counter clockwise. Therefore the system causes the craft to escape from the gravity pull. The craft itself due to this system still has internal gravity because it still has the same weight that it had in the beginning.

L.J. - What charges this battery?

O.T.C. - This starts out electrochemically the same as other batteries, but we do have a regenerating system that is very unique. We are able here, the first time to our knowledge, to use atmospheric electricity as a recharging system. This is done as a part of operational principal of the craft.

L.J. You say you use atmospheric electricity. What happens when you use the atmospheric and there isn't any atmosphere?

O.T.C. - We have electrochemical systems to provide us with all the energy that we need and have a regenerating system in the manner of a regenerative coil that recharges this battery, in the same manner that the storage battery in the automobile is recharged now, by a generator.

L.J. - What you have done is made the first perpetual motion machine.

O.T.C. - There is nothing perpetual about our machine. The energies which cause it to operate are perpetual. You cannot destroy matter, you cannot destroy energy. Molecular flow is perpetual and has been proven in the laboratory. It has been proven that electricity itself is immortal. When we take away resistance we can set up a spark of electricity and it will continue to operate, therefore we have perpetual energy. No machine that we can conceive of made by man would be perpetual, but it is free energy. It's self energizing and as long as all parts function and do not wear out this is truly a self energizing machine.

Ben - About this formula, were you using conventional algebraic methods?

O.T.C. - No, we weren't, partially conventional, but we were joining actual space forms. We arrived at satisfactory equations for ourselves which can be demonstrated.

Ben - Are the physical laws upon which your invention works, are they expressible in mathematical terms?

O.T.C. - Possibly, but I wouldn't say that I'm qualified. We're satisfied with this formula.

Ben - Well, it's like saying plus four divided by minus four equals four.

O.T.C. - Sometimes these solutions are not always what they appear. As we know, in synergy, we know one plus one equals three.

Ben - One plus one equals three? How?

O.T.C. - Because two conditions always produce a third.

Ben - The third condition is two isn't it?

O.T.C. - Not necessarily...

Ben - Could you go over these conditions?

O.T.C. - If one condition operates one way and another operates another way, and when they join you have another condition and their sum is three.

Ben - Well that's a little bit over my head, I've been looking at this prototype you have here and I noticed a wooden frame or scaffolding, you have a larger model of.....that you have in it a turbine and around it is a wooden ring and it seems to be filled with electro-magnets.

O.T.C. - That's right, this is a wood model of the operational model. What we have here is the cones - our Utron electric accumulator - that is the power system. This system activates the electo-magnets and in turn activates...

Ben - Does the system - the thing inside - activate the electro-magnets on the outside?

O.T.C. - This is true. We do this by contacting this lead wire from the positive and negative poles of these batteries to the electro-magnets and then we have circuit breakers from these electro-magnets and we have counter-rotation. These electro-magnets will rotate counter clockwise while the internal area is rotating clockwise.

Ben - Are the spools of wire on the model itself, are they magnetized also?

O.T.C. - The coils of wire inside the ring are regenerative coils, they are electro-motive force coils and they assist the regenerating of the battery. Because they are loops of wire brought through a magnetic field which sets up an electro-motive force. These others are capacitor plates and these are also activated by the central power core; but these plates, which can accept a very high charge in neutral conductance also through the process of ionization utilize atmospheric electricity.

Ben - I mean if you turn that thing...I don't see how you can get a square.

O.T.C. - Dimensionally it is, it is square in these dimensions and when this rotation starts and builds up to a certain velocity, this form is very important because we have the total equation of action and reaction. Now this is done by a system of coil winding wherein we start at a point, expand to an equator, continue our winding down to a point. With this physical expansion and contraction, is an electromagnetic field. Where gravity enters the picture in the form of this relative rotation. When the relative rotation reaches the inertial effective mass, it's a matter of dimension. So that if the earth as we say is 8000 miles in diameter, we know its fixed rotation is one in 24. If we were one mile in diameter its rotation would be 8000 in 24. And by the same system, our 45 foot craft would have a rotation of 580 rpms a minute and when it reaches this rotation it is totally independent of its inertial attractive mass, in an electro-magnetic field.

Ben - 580 rpms a minute, that's not very fast is it?

O.T.C. - Well, if you say a merry-go-round going 580 rpms a minute that would be quite fast.

Ben - If your models get up to 580 rpms a minute, will they take off?

O.T.C. - This model was spun at 40,000 rpms a minute and when it did it set a pressure pattern of 1000 tons, the horsepower reading was a little over 700. Six engineers checked this out. Now the relative rotation of this model would be about 68,000 rpms a minute and when it reaches this rotation, it would immediately take off.

L.J. - Sam Vanderburt is the photographer who took pictures here this morning. They will appear in edition of *Argosy Magazine* dated April 1958.

L.J. - A question from a telegram - Would the time factor be involved with this craft?

O.T.C. - In our solar system, the time factor would be involved, yes. We evaluate time on the velocity of light and in certain systems, if we exceed the velocity of light, unquestionably the time would slow up.

Ben - Your craft can exceed the velocity of light?

O.T.C. - We don't say this, I say in other systems.

Ben - I thought nothing could do this, I thought it was a constant factor, one of Einstein's factors.

O.T.C. - Possibly in our system, but not necessarily true in other systems.

Ben - Anything approaching the speed of light becomes pure energy.

O.T.C. - Pure energy, but in other systems it could change.

Ben - What other systems?

O.T.C. - Other solar systems, we are completely controlled by our system and here the velocity of light is our yardstick and our pattern and our craft is designed around this...

Ben - You just don't upset one of the basic principles of the universe.

Mel Salomey - Doesn't Einstein say any measurement is relative?

Ben - Except this one, it's the first axiom.

Mel - What is an axiom?

Ben - Self-evident truth.

Mel - Thank you. Wasn't Einstein theorizing, wasn't he assuming?

O.T.C. - However we have to get back to what has been accomplished. We have invented an electrified system which makes it possible for a propulsion system which put into operation can carry human beings, with a fuel system which is not expendable and take them into space and bring them back and return in this craft. If I had the tools now, and those tools are available in large plants. If those tools were available to me we could have this craft on the moon in six months from this date.

Question - Mr. Carr, on this sheet I have in front of me, the sheet headed, Performance Characteristics and Delivery Terms for the OTC-X1 circular foil spacecraft. I noticed the paragraph headed 'physical components.' Safety under normal conditions would be anticipated in flight. It would be within 1000 miles away from earth. Now maybe I am not reading this correctly. Sir, but as I read this you are saying that at the present time you feel that the OTC-X1 craft could go a distance of 1000 miles away from earth and yet a few minutes ago you told us you could go to the moon in five hours.

O.T.C. - That is true, the same craft, after all this is a contract form and we have not been to the moon. We are going to enjoy looking at the earth 1000 miles out and I think that would be satisfactory if we make a safe return.

Question - From a thousand miles?

O.T.C. - 1000 miles was picked as an arbitrary figure for demonstration purposes only. Before we delivered the craft we would take the crew a distance of 1000 miles.

Question - Before you delivered to the purchaser?

O.T.C. - That's right.

Question - Then let me ask you Mr. Colton, how long would it take you to go 1000 miles and return provided you don't hover around 1000 miles away from the earth?

Colton - It could be done in a matter of minutes, probably because of the takeoff and landing practicalities, it could be done comfortably in the space of one hour.

Question - Comfortably?

Colton - So as to avoid awkward velocities and any discomforts.

Question - In other words, the possibility of going to the moon in five hours is a dream at the moment, right?

Colton - No, I wouldn't say it's a dream...

Question - Well, if it takes you an hour to go 1000 miles away from earth it should take you a little longer than five to go to the moon unless you've got an indirect route that will save a little time.

Colton - If you think of it in terms of a passenger train leaving a station and arriving at another station or an aircraft traveling between cities. This proportion and the amount of time it takes for takeoff and landing, the distance of approximately 50 miles in a heavy atmosphere would be traveled very slowly. Once out of that atmosphere as Mr. Carr said almost any type of speed is possible up to and approaching the speed of light. You couldn't approach any such speed because you could reach 1000 miles in the wink of an eye. That's why I say the figures are rounded off and arbitrarily selected for discussion and preparing the contract proposal.

Question - Mr. Colton, 20 million dollars sounds like a lot of money if you purchased an amount of jellybeans but it doesn't sound like a lot of money to me if you could produce the craft you propose. Do you have any idea in your mind why some big aeronautical concerns, Lockheed, etc.; I don't know all of them, why it is that they haven't taken advantage of this opportunity to invest. It's quite possible it wouldn't cost them 20 million dollars because they already have so much equipment available to them.

Colton - Up to the present time we haven't approached them directly with an offer.

Question - You were incorporated in 1955 and I imagine you have made an effort to get some money to promote your product.

Colton - An offer we made was that the OTC-X1 craft will be parked in any specified area in the Continental US and go one or more times outside the earth's atmosphere and land within a distance of the Pentagon building in Washington or any other location best suited for public observation.

Question - What are these coils? To describe this the best I can, imagine if you will a circle about 16-18 inches in diameter. Two circles that form a sort of a...in other words 1 circle fits over another circle and from the top of the circle and coming down from off the circle are two cones, in other words one is up like a round pyramid, the other an inverted round pyramid. There are a number of what appears to be copper wound coils around the edge of it. If you looked at it head on it would look like an old fashioned airplane engine more or less. And then there's sort of a framework on top and underneath there's sort of braces. That's the general idea, I noticed this, these cones placed mouth to mouth with some coils, the coils on the edge of this thing, it revolved within this structure. A tough thing to describe.

Question - What is this over here, Mr. Colton?

Colton - This is a paper mockup to show the counter rotation principle and its outside circular section that Roy is describing looking at the other mockup. It contains the electrified horseshoe magnets. This would rotate in one direction counter clockwise while the center section with the electron accumulator would, which he described as two inverted cones mouth to mouth, would rotate clockwise in the other direction.

Question - Would these coils in the outer rim...?

Colton - Rotate counter clockwise, correct.

Question - What is the material in the actual space craft?

Colton - A number of materials would be used.

Question - Was the outer shell possibly aluminum, sir?

Colton - Possibly aluminum, possibly fiberglass. Certainly not any material or materials or products not known to use or easily available.

Question - When you say 580 rpms do you mean the outer rim is rotating in 1 direction 580 rpms and the inner rotating in the other direction at the same speed, giving a total rotation, one relative to the other of 1160 rpms?

Colton - Exactly, although I don't know if 1160 has any bearing on it or not.

Question - Well, it would be twice the rotation in reference to the earth.

Colton - We're not giving it for a certain rotation for the sake of rotation but for the sake of relativity to the attractive mass. The earth at 8000 miles diameter rotating once in 24 hours is relatively equal to a 45 foot craft rotating at 580 and 580 would calculate to be the approximate rotational speed of an automobile tire on a car moving at about 25-30 miles per hour.

L.J. - I'll try to describe a description as seen from the outside. I was attempting to describe the inside of the mechanism which is very difficult but I think I could describe it this way if I may. Imagine taking a couple of loudspeaker cones and putting them mouth to mouth. Now that seems to be the body of the craft as you would see it in flight or well let's say landing. Now around it is an independent ring...so that the mouth to mouth speaker cones revolve inside the ring and on its axis.

Question - It looks like a flying saucer. It sort of reminds me of a gyroscope...

L.J. - Have you described the basic principle of the thing?

Colton - Yes, Mr. Carr described the basic principle and the relationship of electricity and electro-magnetism.

L.J. - Could a small craft be made to take off?

O.T.C. - We plan to build a prototype model as a demonstration device. Now I would like to state certain models have been built by me and tested. Each one has been airborne. One was lost entirely in space. We had a control system and this one didn't function. This has already been done.

L.J. - Years ago a man sold me two pieces of balsa wood, two cross pieces, and a rubber band. It would take off and go up very nicely and gently descend to the ground. It was not surprising to me that a thing like this is quite feasible. As a matter of fact he had a fantastic flying platform. He said it would one day be a way of flying instead of a prop in the front. OK now, how does it differ from this particular flying saucer? That's what it really is, in principle, in motivation. The flying platforms I believe are a combination of a propeller and a jet. Thus directing motion downwards. This does not have anything to do with this system?

Question - None whatsoever. As we calculated, the speed of the circumference was 1263 miles per hour. It gets kind of warm at that, doesn't it?

O.T.C. - No, it won't because it has its own protection field which is its electro-magnetic actuation. We described it as a self contained unit the same as an orange. It contains its juice within its skin and maintains its own circulatory system, like mammals and animals, etc.. This ionization of the capacitor plates sets up a glow brilliantly with a very soft luminescent light.

L.J. - What color?

O.T.C. - It would be in the nature of the blue green or very similar to the electric arc you see in welding. This is the field we are testing, you do not have a heat barrier in forward velocity at all. This electro-magnetic field is being tested out now in conventional aircraft and proved very efficient. We have known that there is something a long time in our particular operation. We found out by actual physical tests.

L.J. - Have you patented this?

O.T.C. - We have patent applications in preparation and on file.

L.J. - I personally am very reluctant to try to argue with you about this device because it looks like a very definite look into the future. Do you think that there are flying saucers from other planets?

O.T.C. - These are electrified unidentified flying objects. We have seen these as mentioned earlier on this program and we were interested inasmuch as we were already building models and tested them out by the time we had these observations. Now, it is not up to me to conjecture whether or not they are from other planets, but the evidence is so because we certainly would not have to spend 355 million dollars to build a rocket if we had such a system, which we propose to make possible. We have the system ourselves. If the system is in operation already, something is very wrong to put this money expense on an expendable rocket. 55 million dollars is no cost at all to test out a rocket that only gets a few feet off the ground.

Question - Well, what do you think about the principle of rockets under certain conditions? Would you suppose you could put rockets toward the edges of the cones and have the ring spin by rocket propulsion?

O.T.C. - We don't need it. We have a tremendous spin here. An electric motor operates the same way. You set up an electromotive force inside a magnetic field and you get rotation. So what we actually have here is an improved electrical motor which in itself is a circular device, and we say we make energy out of the air, from another dimension.

To clear your analogy up also, we would like to demonstrate the fact that this earth itself is literally a spacecraft demonstrating what we're talking about; it's rotating and orbiting at a certain constant speed with a magnetic field and it is in itself a spacecraft.

Question: Mr. Colton, we assume the moon has a gravitational field. How does it make a gravitational field and yet it does not rotate on its axis.

Colton: It does not rotate on its axis?

Question: No, the moon does not rotate on its axis.

Ben: Sure it does, 1 rotation for 1 revolution.

Question: How long does it take?

Ben: 28 days.

Question: And the earth takes one day.

OTC: And that's how engineers and scientists have evaluated the velocity of the craft we call the earth by the orbit of it. Upon the pattern already set up, by the amount of time it takes the moon to rotate once around the earth from the center of the earth's core: 28 days. The distance being 245,000 miles. It is easy to calculate.

Question: These cones seem to revolve over intricately wound copper coils. Do you supply any motor power to this?

OTC: All energy comes from these two cones [Utron]. This in vernacular is a battery. The big novelty is that we have put a battery in motion. We have designed it within the accepted knowledge of total dimensions of space-matter and we have activated it electrochemically [electrolyte in the hollow center] and used the force through chemical activation to activate the entire craft, after which we have motion as the feature of this accumulator.

Ben: Mr. Osgood's telegram brought up a very important and perhaps crucial point, mainly, James Clerk Maxwell demonstrated that light is an electromagnetic radiation, also verified by Hertz who laid the foundation for modern radio. Now the speed of electromagnetic radiation such as radio waves also travels 186,000 miles per second. In other words, light and all forms of electromagnetic radiation travel at the speed of 186,000 miles per second. Now if it were possible for your craft to travel faster than the speed of light, it could, therefore, travel faster than the speed of electromagnetic radiation. So once it exceeded 186,000 miles per second, you wouldn't be gaining all this energy from this electromagnetic radiation you're generating and wouldn't you fall rapidly down?

OTC: There is a continuous falling in space which in itself can bring velocity and can bring you to another system. We mentioned conjecturally that in other systems, there could be different velocities. We're not applying them to our craft. We don't identify them wit our craft. Relatively, we could not go faster than the speed of light unless we were in a system that permitted it. In our solar system, which we have mentioned now three times, it is designed on known principles. We conjectured about other systems.

If we go beyond the speed of light in other systems the conditions within that system would make it possible for us to have power.

Roy: Let's assume, Mr. Carr, this vehicle is at rest. What is it that originally overcomes the inertia of this rotor and starts the rotor moving?

OTC: The electromagnetic force stored in the energy of the Utron electric-accumulator, which in vernacular is a battery.

Roy: Now the Utron electric accumulator is these cones that are inverted to each other with bases together. I know of zinc batteries, nickel-cadmium, lead-acid cells. Could you use those?

OTC: We could use any of the kinds you mentioned; what we have here is tremendous power size in comparison to other batteries; therefore, it's very easy to put 1,000 2-volt cells inside this one unit as you see it. It has functioned very well. In our 45-foot craft we plant to have 12,000-volt batteries which will extend an electromotive force which will energize the electromagnets and the capacitor plates. The generative coils will put back into the batteries in this system the same amount of volts going out until there is a breakdown of electro-chemicals or wear-out of equipment. But it could last as long as average storage batteries in automobiles.

Roy: In order to start the motor off originally, is it necessary to cause a flow of electricity through one set of the coils?

OTC: That's true.

Roy: Is there any magnetic force in the other set of coils at this point?

OTC: They individually operate by circuit breakers and the first motion begins to start a repetition. The same we have in a motor that has the opposite of a commutator, which is an accumulation of contact points where each coil is energized as the current flows through this coil. Then this starts the motion, the repetition of this motion brings the whole motor into phase in the same sense our accumulator and magnets become speeded up and the circuits are made and broken as they rotate.

Roy: Where the inner rotor rotates in one direction and the outer in the other direction. and if the cabin is located on top of the rotating mechanism, what keeps it from rotating in one direction or the other?

OTC: We have this cabin as the center of the craft and the battery below the cabin and the electromagnets are the total outside of the circular foil. The shaft of the accumulator goes through the cabin and there is a bearing. Now, just as this stays stationary when this is rotated, so will the cabin because there are two rotating forces. You have the clockwise rotation of the accumulator, the capacitor plates, the generative coils, you have a counter-rotation of the entire circular area of the craft, the larger diameter which houses the electromagnets; therefore, when you have rotation in both directions, the cabin itself is like a bearing and extension of the shaft. We've built models and proved this is correct.

Roy: OTC-X1 was accomplished?

OTC: Six crafts were airborne, one escaped; we used circuit breakers of various types and fuses burned through the switch and we lost one craft.

Roy: What was the size?

OTC: The largest and the one lost was six feet in diameter.

Roy: You also talk of the Caroto Gravity Motor and you mention it requires no fixed location in which to function, and you also say a lot of other wonderful things about the possibility for this motor. Is it something else than the spacecraft?

OTC: They are two separate packages. The spacecraft utilizes the electrical accumulator and the gravity motor uses the energy of the inertial attractive forces. We have learned how to take this energy and key it to a working shaft and get work power which we call free energy because it is. We don't make any part of it. Now in the rather vulgar vernacular sense this would have been classified as perpetual motion. It is nothing of the sort. It's free energy. Now we have learned that all masses that are smaller than the masses to which they are attracted exert energy. Even this ashtray; if it takes a pound of energy to lift it, then it is exerting a pound of energy. We have a true gravity motor. Its functional operation is to produce power continuously without any dissipation of the energy which causes it to operate, and we have built models of this and they operate and function and we are in the patent procedure with this.

Mel: Back to a question a while ago regarding an analogy of the earth as a spacecraft. Taking another look at the mock up prototype power package there in front of you. It resembles the solar system itself, and as a matter of fact one of the statements in the brochure published in 1957, stated it illustrated the geometry of the universe. It seems that this device miniaturizes and essentially duplicates the motion of bodies in the solar system. It must have the ability to miniaturize their energy. So in a sense, the bodies in the solar system, in all time, have maintained their constant motion perpetually in those motions and this is why people characterize this power package as a perpetual motion machine.

OTC: But we do not make any such claim.

Colton: The Utron has many applications, has many forms, many variation. In one sense you might describe it as an energized armature or in other words a motor with a self-contained moving battery, also capable of continuously re-energizing itself. The offer in regards to spacecraft applies to government and industry alike. We will only make total disclosure demonstration after we have procured a firm order. In other words, we're not looking for anyone to evaluate our development. Mr. Carr has come a long way in his research. He doesn't need any risk money from taxpayers or industries for further exploration and development. We will disclose to anyone who is a purchaser, but not to anyone who comes along for curiosity.

Mel: What does the word "Utron" mean?

Colton: "Utron" is a coined word, a word Mr. Carr put together: the letter "U" and "tron", U meaning the direction or shape of motion as applied and used and equated in this accumulator or battery we described – U is the plane, the geometrical figure that is the portrait of the wave, you might say. The letter U as described on paper, the two-dimensional, is a portrait on paper of the wave or the wave motion with the cut field, with the straight line, the pressure energy in the Utron accelerator.

OTC: To me there's no such thing as a completed curve; you only go half way, just like you only go half way into the woods, then you're coming out. This is the same. A bisection of a total sphere is its exact curve and one-half of it is primarily U-shaped. Because in magnets there are always two poles and one normal way to show them is in a U-shape, but if it's in a bar magnet, there are still two poles and the shape is still the same. We can only put a rope one-half way around the tree and it's coming back the other way, and this is true in all wave motion. Now, if you extend this into velocity, this is the pattern in the sine wave and definitely the electromagnetic wave.

Ben: I see... the vortexian of the wave.

OTC: All motion is relative to all other motion, so this serpentine, spiral state.

Ben: So it's not the form of that motion, the graph and the equation. I'll accept the fact that it's the form of the Utron motion though.

OTC: Also the form as well in two dimensions is intensified in the geometry of our accumulator.

Question: Why do you refer to this vehicle as a 4th dimensional vehicle?

OTC: Because the geometry of the accumulator is such as the 4th dimension. To me the application of space and time, a vibratory field and electricity as we know it is a vibratory force in motion. This is symbolic of it and when it is activated it becomes such. Now this may be a little bit difficult to understand, but nevertheless the very smallest electronic particles of matter have been shown under the highest type of electron microscope to be one-dimensional squares. To me this is verification that this is truly a space dimension because it is the shape of matter. Without matter you couldn't have space.

Question: I'm holding a thing that looks like two loudspeakers in a simplified form, placed mouth to mouth, two cones mouth to mouth, like two tops together so they have a point at each end and actually like a thickened flying saucer... Now what is it that comes from that: is it a high voltage?

OTC: The voltage is whatever we wish to make it by design.

Question: In other words, then, this is a battery?

OTC: That's right.

Question: The battery then goes through these magnets?

OTC: The battery rotates in this magnetic field. The average armature today in any electrical system is usually the permeability, iron wound with copper, then through a magnetic field acts as a motor, or it becomes a generator, depending upon the lead. The great novelty here in the area in which an armature is normally used, we have a [power unit, and this a battery, and this is a moving power unit.

Question: In other words, you might call this a self-contained power supply, right? How would this generator --- maybe I'm using the wrong word --- gather additional energy from outside?

OTC: This is due to its circular motion. Electrical forces are motions where they manifest. Now we have cycles in alternating current; AC gives you 60 cycles per second; we have discovered in our experiments that there is a space cycle related to electricity, and if we join the cycle we get energy from it.

Question: Mr. Colton, will you try to describe to our listeners how they can draw at home a facsimile of an Utron?

Colton: You can take a pencil and draw four lines to form an open square. When you have a square, draw a straight line from one point of the square to an opposite point and you'll have two right angle triangles. Now if you convert the line you've just drawn into a small lip you'll begin to see two inverted cones, the base of which form a circular equator. While you started with a square, you now have two cones. Obviously, the base of the cone is a circle or completely round as we describe it, and you have the device which is described as completely round and completely square, the Utron electric accumulator. The cavity in the center of these which is a hemisphere when the two cones are put together have a hollow sphere. This is the cavity which contains the electrolyte which would be used in some of the applications of the accumulator.

Question: Of what value is the term "completely round and completely square" apart from its obvious redundancy?

Colton: It is Carr's definition of the geometry or the basic space form or the basic form of all matter large or small relatively as we describe it. It is the definition of the terminal motions of universal energies in what we call space.

Question: In one of your brochures you make mention of a "photon gun" and you say, "This is primarily a development that works outside of the earth's atmosphere. We are entering an age of space flight and the use of solar energy is practically unlimited"... What is a photon gun?

OTC: I am using the word "gun" as a reaction principle instead of as a weapon. Nevertheless, it is a gun and in fact fires billions of rays of solar energy at right angles to the reception. By placing them through a certain chamber, we have been able to get a reaction and whenever there is a reaction, we can get power, we can get force from it. So we feel outside the earth's atmosphere new systems of propulsion even beyond our own of electromagnetism will make themselves apparent.

* * *

Public Relations Showing of OTC-X1 Model

The First Civilian Spacecraft

ACCORDING to Otis Carr, "Any vehicle accelerated to an axis rotation relative to its attractive inertial mass, immediately becomes activated by free-space-energy and acts as an independent force... We have shown that a charged body, accelerated to an axis rotation relative to this attractive inertial mass, indicates polarity in a given direction.

"The dip-needle points, say, up toward the top of the body. But mount this while rotating body, with its spindle, on another platform and rotate this platform on a spindle, then if the counter-rotation is greater than the inertial forward rotation of the body, a dip-needle on the second platform will point down while the first dip-needle points up, indicating complete relativity of polarity. When the exact counter-rotation matches the forward rotation the body loses its polarity entirely and immediately becomes activated by free energy (tensor stresses in space) and acts as an independent force... The above-described assembly of counter-rotating charged masses becomes weightless and will escape the immediate attraction of gravitational forces."

Carr's engine had only two moving parts – like two spinning tops on top of one another, each spinning in a different direction. Carr stated that, "when counter-rotation matches' forward rotation, a body loses its polarity... and creates a kind of independent force. This causes the counter-rotating mass to escape the full effect of gravitational influence."

Similar results, pertaining to the apparent antigravitic properties of rotating objects, have been shown by a variety of researchers – most notably, the eminent British engineer Professor Eric Laithwaite, who demonstrated an apparent loss of weight in a sealed system containing an arrangement of spinning gyroscopes and called upon the scientific community to research the phenomenon. Intriguingly, the "Jell-o" description of the altered state of solid metal, attained under specific and unusual conditions, has also been reported by the researcher John Hutchison, and is part of the lore of The Philadelphia Experiment.

Carr said that his vehicle was actually finished in 1947, but at the time he was unable to generate any interest in it. Carr stated that the core of his space ship would be a huge battery which would spin at the velocity of the external craft and which would be recharged by its own motion. Carr went on to declare that such a battery, built to any size, could be designed to power the largest electric generating plant, operate an automobile, heat a house or power any conceivable machine or device.

Carr did manage to get a patent granted at the U.S. Patents Office for an "Amusement Device" US Patent #2,912,224 - filed January 22, 1959. The U.S. Patent and Trademark Office will not issue a patent for a "flying saucer" or any other type of levitating disk. The patent application had to be written as something else to satisfy the patent office. Otis T. Carr added some extra text to call it an amusement device.

In 1958, Carr worked out a deal with Frontier City, an amusement park in Oklahoma City, Oklahoma. The terms of the deal were that Carr would construct a full-scale (45 ft) mockup of his OTC-X1 saucer, to be converted into a ride for the park. Carr relocated to Oklahoma City, provided the park with a dummy OTC-X1, and claimed to be readying a 6-foot "prototype" of his saucer for a demonstration flight at the fairground. Carr said his demonstration model would rise to about 500 feet.

As well, Major Wayne Aho, a former Army Combat Intelligence Officer during World War II, announced that he would take the OTC-X1 on a five-hour trip to the moon on December 7, 1959. The 45 diameter craft he was to use weighed 30 tons and "was powered by the Utron engine."

On April 15, 1959, a launch event in Oklahoma City was held with hundreds of people invited to view the event. After several hours delay, an announcement stated that the launch was postponed due to a badly engineered bearing. Long John Nebel, who had traveled all the way from New York City to view the event, finally managed to locate Carr at the nearby Mercy hospital. Carr had been admitted into the hospital for with a lung hemorrhage. In addition, in a preliminary pre-flight test, the accumulator had developed a leak which had sprayed mercury over the inside mechanism.

Unfortunately, the event was never rescheduled and the 6-foot prototype of the OTC-X1 was never delivered to Frontier City, causing the authorities to start an investigation on Carr and OTC Enterprises. It was reported that visitors to Carr's factory did not see any actual working models of either the 6-foot or the 45-foot saucers. Instead, they were shown a small and motionless "three dimensional illustration of Carr's ideas" made mainly of wood.

One Oklahoma City television reporter expressed the general feeling of the townspeople, "This thing will never leave the ground, and I feel that a great deal of the ballyhoo they're giving out is tied in with the ride at Frontier City. I have tried constantly to get in to see the saucer model, but they've kept it hidden."

With growing hostile public opinion in Oklahoma, Carr decided to move his center of operations to Apple Valley, California in late 1959. To prevent any further public debacles, he decided not to announce any test flights in advance. With new financial backing and a large production plant, Osbrink, at his disposal, Carr proceeded with his plans to develop and test his spacecraft.

In raising revenue for his spacecraft program, Carr was experiencing increasing problems with the U.S. Securities and Exchange Commission that had placed an injunction against Carr, ordering him to cease selling unregistered stock."

On June 2, 1960, Carr told an audience of 300 people that it was a "treacherous misstatement of fact to say or infer that we [OTC Enterprises] are coming to California to raise money in stock sales." The U.S. Securities and Exchange Commission had placed an injunction against Carr, ordering him to cease selling unregistered stock. Negative publicity began to appear in various publications, and there were hints of impropriety, though never with any proof, other than the fact that no working model of the OTC-X1 was ever shown publicly.

In January 1961, the Attorney General of New York, Louis J. Lefkowitz, stated that Carr had swindled $50,000, and later that year *True Magazine* labeled him a hoaxer. By then, his laboratory had been raided and destroyed, and the group of engineers had been ordered to disband and cease contact with one another. It is not known what became either of Carr himself or the craft... but they never flew again. Carr is reported to have suffered from ill health, a broken man. He passed away in Gardnerville, Nevada, in 2005.

The authorities and the press labeled Otis T. Carr as a charlatan, out to make a quick buck off the gullible. However, years later, a man named Ralph Ring emerged claiming that he knew the truth about Carr and the suppression of the first civilian spacecraft.

In March 2006, Ring came forward to reveal that he was one of three pilots of a successful test of Carr's full scale prototype of the OTC-X1. Ralph Ring claimed to be a technician who was recruited into Carr's team attempting to build a 45-foot prototype spacecraft after Carr had relocated in California in 1959.

According to Michael E. Salla, PhD. In his article: *How the U.S. Government Suppressed the World's First Civilian Spacecraft Industry*, Ring at the time was an engineer who had grown frustrated with corporate sector disinterest in innovative principles concerning electromagnetic energy. He had earlier helped the famous French oceanographer Jacques Cousteau develop the aqualung, and later worked at a government-funded research organization called Advanced Kinetics.

In a series of public interviews and presentations, Ring described the conditions of leaving Advanced Kinetics. He claims to have resolved two complex engineering problems involving electromagnetism. Confident of a job promotion, Ring was instead told by the director that they were a government funded corporation and "we're paid to look for the answers, but not to find them!" In frustration, Ring left and met with Carr in late 1959, and was quickly impressed with his ideas, including a plan to build a civilian spacecraft.

In his first public interview, Ring described Carr as follows: "He was an unquestioned genius. Tesla had recognized his quality immediately and had taught him everything he knew. He was inspired, and – like Tesla – seemed to know exactly what to do to get something to work. He was a private man and was also very metaphysical in his thinking. I think the fact that he was not formally trained in physics helped him. He was not constrained by any preconceived ideas. As crazy as it sounds now, he was determined to fly to the moon and really believed it could be done. I believed it. We all did."

Ring directly participated in the testing of smaller models of the OTC-X1 craft developed by Carr. He described how these had been successfully tested and exhibited unique characteristics when achieving certain rotational speeds: "...the metal turned to Jell-o. You could push your finger right into it. It ceased to be solid. It turned into another form of matter, which was as if it was not entirely here in this reality. That's the only way I can attempt to describe it. It was uncanny, one of the weirdest sensations I've ever felt."

Even more incredible is that Ring claims that the 45-foot OTC-X1 prototype developed by Carr was completed and successfully tested back in 1959. Ring says he was one of three pilots on the craft which flew 10 miles instantaneously. Ring described how Carr had been able to maintain communications with the three man team piloting the OTC-X1 who were instructed to complete a series of tasks, before returning to the launch site.

When asked if the OTC-X1 had flown to its destination, Ring said: "Fly is not the right word. It traversed distance. It seemed to take no time. I was with two other engineers when we piloted the 45' craft about ten miles. I thought it hadn't moved – I thought it had failed. I was completely astonished when we realized that we had returned with samples of rocks and plants from our destination. It was a dramatic success. It was more like a kind of teleportation."

Ring described how the test flight had been able to change the flow of time: "What's more, time was distorted somehow. We felt we were in the craft about fifteen or twenty seconds. We were told afterwards that we'd been carefully timed as having been in the craft no longer than three or four minutes. I still have no complete idea how it worked."

The most remarkable part of Ring's testimony concerns the unique navigation system used by the pilots to control the movements of the OTC-X1. According to Ring, this navigation system used the conscious intent of the pilots rather than conventional technology.

"The Utron was the key to it all. Carr said it accumulated energy because of its shape, and focused it, and also responded to our conscious intentions. When we operated the machine, we didn't work any controls. We went into a kind of meditative state and all three of us focused our intentions on the effect we wanted to achieve. It sounds ridiculous, I know.

"But that's what we did, and that's what worked. Carr had tapped into some principle which is not understood, in which consciousness melds with engineering to create an effect. You can't write that into equations. I have no idea how he knew it would work. But it did."

Success of the first test of the full scale OTC-X1 meant that planning for flights into outer space and to the moon was now proceeding in earnest. Ring said Carr and his crew worked round the clock to complete the testing program before announcing the results to the general public.

Ring continues with the shocking revelation that two weeks after the successful test of the OTC-X1, Carr's operation was closed down by the FBI and other government agencies. This secret raid involved seven or eight truckloads of armed government personnel. The FBI told Carr that his project was being closed "because of your threat to overthrow the monetary system of the United States of America."

Indeed, Carr's successful testing of a civilian spacecraft, had it been allowed to go ahead, would have revolutionized the energy sector and the aerospace industry. The conventional energy industry using fossil fuels to generate electric power and the aviation industry would have become redundant overnight. Large U.S. corporate interests in the energy sector would have lost their substantial investments. Lack of corporate profits would throw countless thousands out of work.

The financial effect of a civilian spacecraft industry using electrical energy from the atmosphere for power would indeed have placed enormous pressure on the U.S. monetary system possibly causing its collapse.

In a series of interviews and public presentations, Ring claims FBI agents confiscated all the equipment including the OTC-X1 prototype. They debriefed all of Carr's employees, warned them to remain silent on what had happened, and made Carr sign non-disclosure agreements. Ring's testimony, if true, reveals what really happened with Otis Carr's radical civilian spacecraft project. Rather than Carr being a fraud who deceived a number of investors funding his radical civilian spacecraft ideas, Carr had been successful.

His success so threatened entrenched interests in the energy sector, that his operation was shut down with the full approval and knowledge of a select number of government agencies concerned with the financial impact on the U.S. monetary system. Carr himself was forced to endure trumped up charges designed to discredit him, and end his bold effort to develop a civilian spacecraft industry.

There is no doubt that Ralph Ring is telling the truth. He has provided a number of photographs of the OTC-X1 that had not previously been published. The photos showed that Carr had indeed succeeded in building a number of models including the 45-foot prototype spacecraft. The photos dispel the view that Carr had not succeeded in developing a full-scale prototype spacecraft. Ring's photos are material evidence that he did indeed collaborate with Carr on the OTC-X1, as he claims.

Perhaps most significant is what occurred to Ring soon after coming forward to reveal his experiences with Otis Carr in March 2006. Bill Ryan, one of the founders of Project Camelot describes what happened:

"Shortly afterwards, Ralph went into the hospital for a routine knee replacement operation. He accidentally received the wrong treatment, and nearly died three times. At the time of writing (July 2006) he has just recently emerged, very frail, from intensive care - but is determined to tell his story. Prior to that he had enjoyed perfect health for 71 years."

In his presentation at the 2007 International UFO Congress, Ring described how he had been taken by ambulance to a hospital 25 miles away, bypassing a hospital adjacent to where he was staying. Ring hovered perilously close to death as a result of the 'mistreatment' and the long ambulance ride.

The circumstances are certainly suspicious and do indicate an effort to silence Ring. This series of "accidental" events that almost took Ring's life soon after his public emergence provides circumstantial evidence in support of his claims. Salla speculates that the reason for the treatment given to Carr and his technicians was that government authorities had no need for Carr's ideas on how to develop a spacecraft capable of light speed, and which could tap into free electrical energy available in the Earth's atmosphere. Responsible government authorities would also have no need for the unique navigation system developed by Carr for his OTC-X1 that used a mind-technology interface between the pilots and the spacecraft.

This was not because government authorities were not interested in these ideas. More likely, these authorities already had a classified project for an antigravity craft capable of near light speed and powered by electrical energy drawn from the natural environment. The principles for 'light speed' space flight were likely so well known that the efforts of civilian inventors were simply not needed in classified antigravity projects.

The conclusion is that in the 1950's, the U.S. government already had a number of operational spacecraft that were capable of attaining near light speed, and could draw electrical energy from the Earth's atmosphere that could be stored for space travel.

A final possible motive for the closing down of Carr's spacecraft program is that an exclusive group of quasi-governmental or "shadow government" authorities with strong ties to corporations did not want to alert regular military and/or government authorities of the existence of such advanced technology.

The theory that the United States already has an operating fleet of antigravity spacecraft is certainly intriguing. As discussed earlier in this book and in Tim R. Swartz's book *The Lost Journals of Nikola Tesla*, Tesla had made important advances in the discovery and understanding of "field propulsion." His research was coveted and stolen by not only Nazi Germany, but by the United States as well.

Nikola Tesla died a broken man, penniless and forgotten. Yet, others became very rich and powerful based on Tesla's stolen research. To this day, Tesla's contributions to science have been marginalized and derided by those who say he was not a true scientist, but simply an engineer who got lucky. In addition, Tesla's name has become associated with metaphysics, extraterrestrials and other over-the-top claims. It may be that this is a deliberate effort at disinformation to dissuade civilian scientists from attempting further research on some of Tesla's ideas such as free energy, the wireless transmission of electricity, and antigravity. Public research along these lines is a guaranteed career-buster.

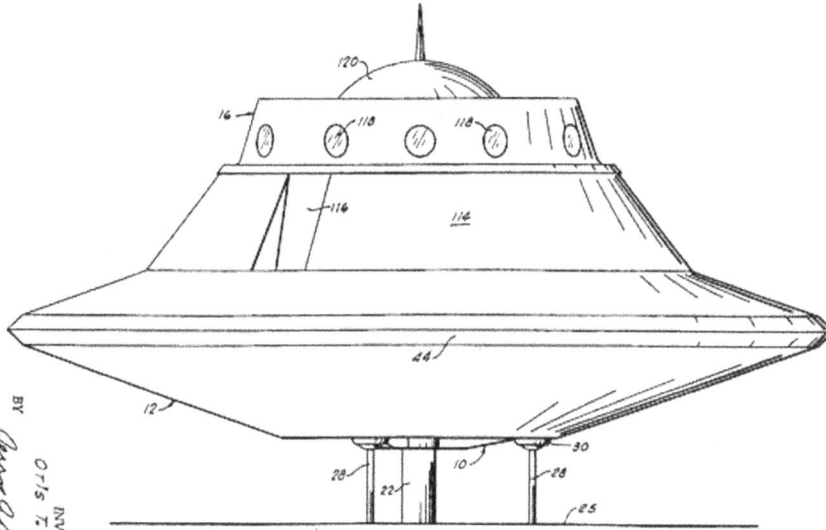

Nov. 10, 1959

Filed Jan. 22, 1959

O. T. CARR

AMUSEMENT DEVICE

2,912,244

5 Sheets—Sheet 1

F1G-1

INVENTOR.
OTIS T. CARR
BY
ATTORNEY

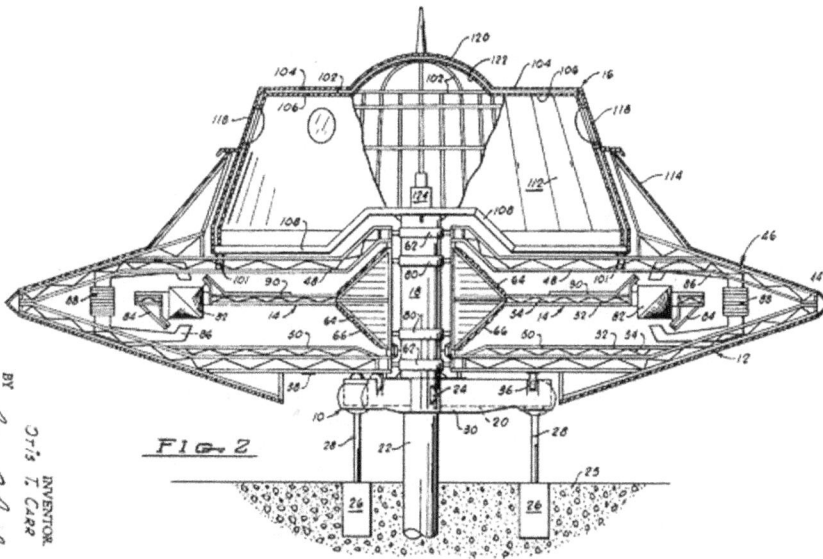

Nov. 10, 1959

Filed Jan. 22, 1959

O. T. CARR

AMUSEMENT DEVICE

2,912,244

5 Sheets—Sheet 2

F1G-2

INVENTOR.
OTIS T. CARR
BY
ATTORNEY

Nov. 10, 1959   O. T. CARR   2,912,244

AMUSEMENT DEVICE

Filed Jan. 22, 1959   5 Sheets-Sheet 3

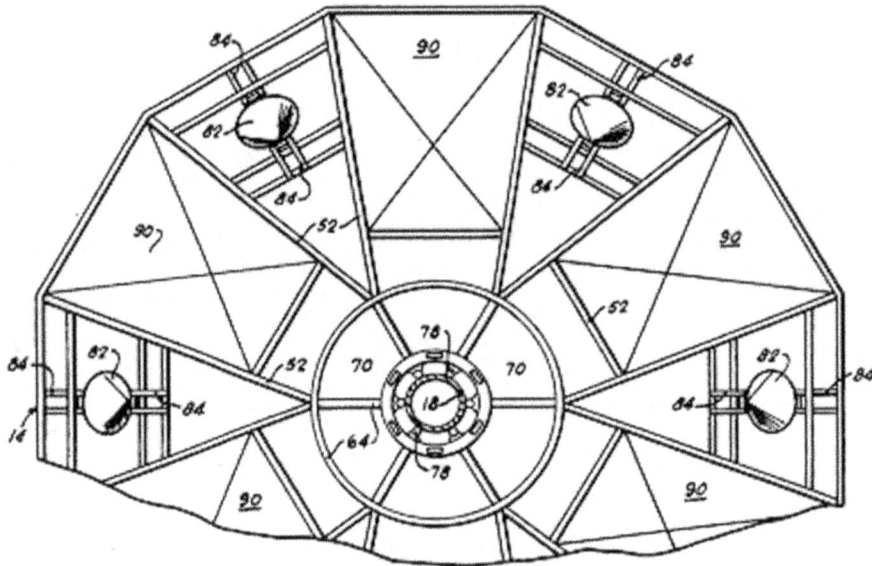

Fig. 5

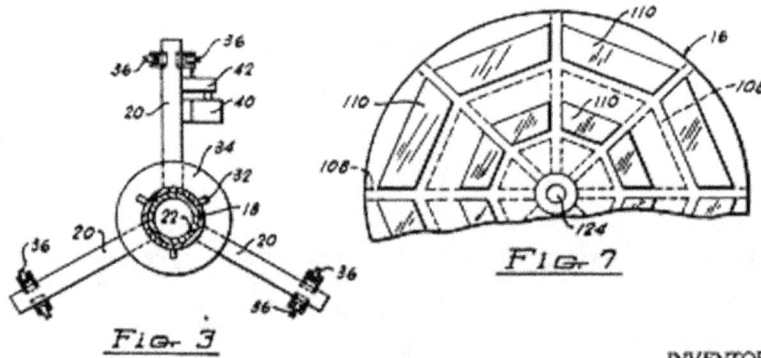

Fig. 3

Fig. 7

INVENTOR.
OTIs T. CARR

BY

Jerry J. Dunlap

ATTORNEY

Above: Model of OTC-X1. Below: Actual OTC-X1 spacecraft from Ralph Ring Photo Collection.

The Secret Space Program and Solar Warden

WERE Otis T. Carr and his team of engineers put out of business because there was already a secret space program based on Tesla technology? There is good evidence that such a program exists, and has been around since at least the early 1950's.

In 1967, Jack Pickett, a publisher of Air Force in-house magazines, was approached by the Adjutant General's Office at MacDill AFB (Tampa, Florida). It was proposed to Pickett that he do an article on the subject of vintage, historical or experimental aircraft. Pickett was told that some experimental jet aircraft were being stored at the base salvage/scrap-yard. These particular aircraft had been decommissioned/declassified, and were parked outside, not in a hangar.

In September, Pickett, along with his partner Harold Baker, drove to where these aircraft were parked. Upon arriving at the chain link fence, which surrounded the perimeter of the base near the scrap-yard, Pickett saw the strangest aircraft he had ever seen. His first thought was, "My gosh! Those are Flying Saucers! Those things really do exist!"

Right in front of their eyes were four disc-shaped aircraft, measuring 20 to 108 feet in diameter. Because they were the last remaining of their model, the Master Sergeant of the Non-Commissioned Officer's Club telephoned the Adjutant General's Office for permission for Polaroid photographs to be taken, even though all of the tires were completely flat down to their wheel rims.

The General's Office (headed by base commander William M. Wilson) suggested that Jack use higher quality official Air Force photographs available at the Adjutant General's library at MacDill. Under armed guard, Pickett was shown hundreds of official USAF photographs of these aircraft in formation flight, on the tarmac, and was shown portions of motion picture footage of these aircraft in flight. Pickett was allowed to select those photographs best suited for the up-coming NCO Club newsletter article, and obtain additional detailed information concerning the discs.

When Pickett first saw the official USAF photos of these aircraft, he was amazed, and immediately asked questions regarding how large, and how many of these aircraft were built. Jack also inquired about the flight performance (altitude and cruise speed) for these aircraft. Some of the in-flight photos clearly showed the discs being escorted by an F-84 Thunderjet (straight-wing) interceptor aircraft. Looking head on, they appeared as the classic so-called "Flying Saucer" shape, very similar to two saucers stacked one over the other.

The pilot/crew compartment appearing as a bubble shaped contour located directly in the middle of the top of the disc. There was nothing forward of the pilot's compartment other than the sloping surface. That compartment tapered back towards the trailing edge of the disc, narrowing down to a high vertical tail. The small 20' diameter craft had a crew of one, with an air-intake on both sides of the pilot's compartment, and two exhaust ports at the aft lower portion of the disc.

This aircraft also employed control surfaces along the circumference of the disc. According to Pickett, the smaller disc seemed to incorporate a sort of magnifying/enlarging optical sight, which was directly embedded into the 1-1/2 to 2" thick canopy windows. The standard Air Force insignia, and the word "XPERIMENTAL" followed by "USAF", was visibly printed starting immediately behind the windows of the compartment on towards the tail.

All four discs were polished aluminum silver in color, with the aircraft skin seams and rivets clearly visible. Amazingly, each aircraft was so exceedingly streamlined that it appeared as though each craft were made out of one piece. The discs themselves, regardless of size, all had tricycle landing gear. The size of the aircraft, determined how many wheels on each. According to the O.I.C. (Officer in charge) of MacDill, all four aircraft had been flown in, and then immediately parked outside at the scrap-yard. The O.I.C. also informed Pickett that no one had been allowed to enter any of the discs since their arrival.

Measuring 108 feet in diameter, and standing 12' off the ground, the largest of the four discs must have been a remarkable sight. The O.I.C. permitted Pickett to walk under and around this aircraft, and was actually allowed to kick the tires of the smaller 40' craft, while the O.I.C. stood nearby and snapped a photo in the process. Pickett specifically noted that the port main landing gear was partially collapsed, causing the aircraft to lean to the left. Each main landing gear consisted of six wheels, measuring 5' in diameter.

The nose gear had an incredible 32 wheels, each measuring 2-1/2 to three feet in diameter. A door was located on the port side of the craft, for access to the crew compartment.

Immediately behind the door, were three windows that ran along both sides of the fuselage. These may have been stations for the flight engineer, navigator, and weapon systems operator. The large craft employed two air-intakes on both sides of the crew compartment, and four exhaust ports at the aft bottom end of the craft. The air intakes blended beautifully into the sides of the fuselage and upper portion of the disc.

Pickett specifically recalls that the unusually high vertical stabilizer was "higher than shopping mall parking lot lights." It was evident that the landing gear retracted inside the main body of the disc, with the gear moving up and away from the centerline of the aircraft. Flight control surfaces were located along the circumference of the disc, similar to the 20' model.

Pickett remembers seeing what may have been bomb bay doors located on the bottom surface of the disc. These may have been used for the release of 10' diameter in-flight radio controlled flying wing disc bomb drones. Indeed, Pickett remembers seeing flying wing disc drones in various stages of disrepair at the scrapyard, near the four discs. These bombs were capable of delivery with "pin-point" accuracy decades before Lockheed F-117 Stealth Fighters dropped "smart bombs" on Iraq during the Gulf War. This indicates that the primary mission for this aircraft may have been that of a long-range reconnaissance bomber. Pickett was told that this aircraft regularly over-flew Russia after WWII, but was told, "you can't print that."

When Pickett asked the O.I.C. if these were the flying saucers everybody was reporting, he was given an affirmative reply. It's clear that what was being reported, was one of the smaller craft, specifically the 40' diameter model. The overall logistics and tremendous costs involved in manufacturing the giant 108' model may have prevented it from being produced in great quantity.

Pickett was never briefed on the exact propulsion system utilized by the four craft, or who specifically built these aircraft. However, Pickett was told that these aircraft could fly so high, and so fast, that they were actually capable of achieving space flight. By definition, that would eliminate conventional jet engines, due to their tendency to "flame-out" at extremely high altitudes. This would mean that these aircraft were capable of literally flying rings around anything operating at the time. With a top speed of 15,500 mph, and an almost unlimited range, they definitely still remain among the utter most classified aircraft in the USAF inventory. Pickett also inquired why they had been discontinued, and was told that it had to do with maneuverability problems, and that the Air Force now had "better ones."

Unfortunately, the four disc shaped experimental aircraft were never featured in the October 1967 issue of *NCO Club News*. Coincidentally, while putting that article together, there was a UFO/Flying Saucer sighting that occurred directly over downtown Miami. That particular aircraft Pickett was told, originated from Avon Park Air Force Range located 100 miles Southeast of MacDill AFB. Avon Park consisted of runways far too short for the operation of conventional high-speed horizontal take-off aircraft. Only "harrier type" or VTOL aircraft would be ideally suited for operations at this facility.

Pickett learned that this new prototype developed a propulsion system malfunction, which caused it to drop down to "tree-top level." Eventually, the flight crew regained control of the aircraft, and quickly departed the Miami. Pickett brought this sighting, which took place during September of 1967 to the attention of the O.I.C. at MacDill, who personally felt that he should make a request to higher Air Force authority for the clearance needed for publication at that time. To Pickett's chagrin, it was decided that it would be in the "better interest of the Air Force" to delay publication of his article.

The remaining secret aircraft at MacDill were more-than-likely dismantled and scrapped. To this day, they remain top-secret due to the continuing development and deployment of their successors. It is clear that these Air Force "flying saucers" were the reason that Otis T. Carr's OTC-X1 spacecraft had been suppressed by the government. The antigravity technology developed by Carr and his engineers must have been close to the technology utilized by the Air Force's flying saucers. This was something that the U.S. could not allow a civilian operation to develop for fear that it would be stolen and used by a hostile foreign power. (Thanks to Jack D. Pickett and Michael H. Schratt for the information contained in this section.)

This brings us to the secret space program its code-name is "Solar Warden." The Solar Warden Space Fleet operates under the

US Naval Network and Space Operations Command (NNSOC) (formerly Naval Space Command), headquartered in Dahlgren, Virginia. There are approximately 300 personnel at NNSOC's Dahlgren facility. The Solar Warden Space Fleet's vessels are staffed by Naval Space Cadre officers, whose training has earned them the prestigious 6206-P Space Operations specialty designation, after they have graduated from advanced education at the Naval Postgraduate School in Monterey, California and earned a Master of Science degree in Space Systems Operations.

The Space Fleet operates not only with classified U.S. Government authority but also with the secret authority of the United Nations, because the Space Fleet's mission is to protect the entire Earth and all countries. When British civilian Gary McKinnon hacked into U.S. Space Command computers several years ago and learned of the existence of "non-terrestrial officers" and "fleet-to-fleet transfers" and a secret program called "Solar Warden," he was charged by the Bush Justice Department with having committed "the biggest military computer hack of all time."

However, bringing McKinnon to open court would involve his testifying to the above classified facts, and his attorney would be able to subpoena government officers to testify under oath about the Navy's Space Fleet. To date the extradition of McKinnon to the U.S. has gone nowhere.

Allegedly, Solar Warden consists of eight ships, an equivalent to aircraft carriers and forty-three "protectors," which are space planes. One was lost recently to an accident in Mars' orbit while it was attempting to re-supply the multinational colony within Mars. This base was established in 1964 by American and Soviet teamwork.

Computer generated images of USAF saucer-shaped aircraft as reported by Jack Pickett. (Graphics by Giesbert Nijhius)

Richard Dolan and the Breakaway Civilization

IN his article for *UFO Digest, Is A "Breakaway Civilization" Behind The Mysterious Secret Space Program?*, UFO journalist Sean Casteel spoke with Richard Dolan, the author of **UFOs And The National Security State**, Volumes I and II. Dolan told Casteel why he believes the rumored secret space program really does exist, saying, "I think that there are a number of anomalous events we know have occurred in Earth orbit and beyond Earth orbit. We've got 40 years of events recorded by US and Soviet astronauts of objects in orbit that appear to be not our own that seemed to move intelligently. We have the evidence of what's known as DSP satellites – that's Defense Support Program satellites. These are a series of geosynchronous satellites in Earth orbit that have a long record of tracking 'fast-walkers' in space. That is, objects that are like a space UFO."

According to Dolan, there have been nearly 300 such anomalous events recorded by the DSP satellites in the years 1973 to 1991.

"It would seem to me very logical," Dolan continued, "that just as there would be a covert monitoring of the UFO phenomenon within Earth's atmosphere and on the ground and so forth, if there are anomalous activities going on in space, then clearly you would want an agency to monitor that as well, to deal with it. And that would necessitate the creation of a very clandestine component to the US space program."

The normally staid Dolan also allows for the possibility of there being an alien and/or human presence on the dark side of the moon that is concealed from public view. The information comes from leaks within the military world that, while not "airtight," are nonetheless credible.

"You get the claim quite a few times," Dolan said, "of NASA airbrushing and doctoring moon photographs. Again, these are claims, but I look at a number of these claims and they strike me as sincere individuals, and, frankly, I have no reason to doubt what they're saying. So that makes me think there's more funny business going on. They're hiding something important about space."

Even Mars is a possible location for artificial structures of some kind, according to Dolan, though he does not lend credence to reports from people who claim to have actually been there. Recovered UFO technology also fits into the mix.

"It makes perfect sense to me," he explained, "when you look at the history of apparent UFO crashes and recoveries, and there are a number I think there are good cases for, you have to assume that the national security apparatus isn't going to be just sitting on their hands looking at this technology forever. Of course they're going to try to study it and obviously to replicate it. How could they not?"

So that allows 40 to 50 years, Dolan continued, with a lot of black budget money and secrecy, in which a classified reverse-engineering group could work.

"And if you've had any success with it," Dolan said, "it's not something you can share with the world. Yet it would be something that would come in very handy for covert missions beyond Earth's orbit, i.e., a secret space program."

Dolan also described something he calls a "breakaway civilization," or a secret group with technological knowledge light years beyond the everyday world.

"I think this is something that is real," Dolan said. "Now, my theory of it is that it originated in really in post-World War II society, but there's nothing preventing such a thing from having happened earlier. The basic idea of the 'breakaway civilization' is simply that you have a secret group, a classified group of people, with access to radically advanced technology, radically advanced science, and they just don't share it with the rest of the world. One scientific breakthrough leads to another, and that leads to another and so on. So the next thing you know, you've got a separate group of humanity that is vastly far beyond the rest of the world."

Conclusion

IN the early 21st century, innovation is touted as the savior of all humanities future. Every year, new technological triumphs for mass consumption are heralded as the "next big thing." The buying public is then expected to run out with credit card in hand to "keep up with the Jones," or risk being left behind by all the "cool" people.

It seems as if innovative technology has been regulated to "gee-whiz" toys such as smart phones, big-screen televisions, tablets, etc. All, it seems, has one goal in mind, keep the general population mindless and sated with meaningless pop culture. It no longer seems to matter that all of our politicians are ultra-rich elitists who get themselves elected by demonizing and bullying the weakest members of our society. Who cares if there are no jobs as long as we stop those horrible same-sex marriages? The ploy is to distract the ignorant from those who control in secret.

Could innovative thinkers such as Nikola Tesla or Otis T. Carr be able to survive in the 21st century? Or, would they, like so many others who have attempted to break the bonds of servitude, end up forever silenced? The human spirit is a hard thing to constrain. Continuously, new paradigms of thought are able to break free of restrictions and censorship. Yet it seems that for every forward step we manage to take, the powers-that-be forces us to take three steps back.

The truth about the amazing inventions of Nikola Tesla and Otis T. Carr may never come out. There may simply be too much money and power involved to ever allow the world to know the incredible things that could be made possible by utilizing the technology first conceived by these amazing individuals.

If this is the case, then Nikola Tesla and Otis T. Carr will forever remain...men of mystery.

United States Patent Office
Patent issue date
Nov. 10, 1959
2,912,244
AMUSEMENT DEVICE
Otis T. Carr, Baltimore Md.
Application January 22, 1959, Serial No. 788,392
9 Claims - (CL 272-18)

This invention relates generally to improvements in amusement devices, and more particularly, to an improved amusement device of the type wherein the passengers will receive the impression of riding in an interplanetary space craft.

The present invention contemplates a novel amusement device having the overall configuration of a space craft and being formed in various sections with portions of the sections being rotated in opposite directions to give the impression of movement to the passengers. It is also contemplated to move the craft up and down and display an animated movie of heavenly bodies above the passengers to give the passengers and impression of leaving the Earth and approaching a distant planet or the like. This invention further contemplates the provision of electro-magnets, cones and the like carried by the oppositely rotating sections of the device, and windows through which the passengers may view these simulated objects to give the impression to the passengers that they are viewing the inner workings of an interplanetary space craft during flight of the craft. Finally, this invention contemplates the construction of the various portions of an amusement device simulating an interplanetary space craft in such a manner that the device may be easily transported in sections from one location to another and reassembled in a minimum of time.

An important object of this invention is to provide and amusement device wherein a passenger in the device receives the impression of flying in an interplanetary space craft.

Another object of this invention is to provide and amusement device having a general configuration of an interplanetary space craft and having oppositely rotating sections simulating the movement of various portions of such a space craft during flight.

A further object of this invention is to provide a portable amusement device simulating an interplanetary space craft which may be easily disassembled and transported from one location to another.

Still further object of this invention is to provide an amusement device which is simple in construction, may be economically manufactured, and which will have a long service life.

Other objects and advantages of the invention will be evident from the following detailed description, when read in conjunction with the accompanying drawings which illustrate my invention.

In the drawings:

Figure 1 is an elevational view of and amusement device constructed in accordance with this invention.

Figure 2 is a vertical section view through the device illustrated in Fig. 1.

Figure 3 is a plan view of the landing gear for the amusement device, with the housing around the legs of the landing gear removed.

Figure 4 is a plan view of the supporting structure or frame work for the outer rotating shell of the amusement device shown in Fig. 1 and 2.

Figure 5 is a plan view of the central rotating assembly which rotates within the outer shell frame illustrated in Fig. 2 and 4.

Figure 6 is an enlarged sectional view illustrating the support and drive between the inner rotating assembly.

Figure 7 is a plan view of the floor portion of the passenger cabin.

Referring to the drawings in detail, and particularly Figs. 1 and 2, a preferred embodiment of the present invention comprises, generally speaking, a supporting structure and landing gear 10, and outer rotating shell 12, and inner rotating assembly 14 and a passenger cabin 16 extending downwardly into the upper end portion of the outer shell 12. The landing gear and supporting mechanism 10 comprises a vertically extending tubular member 18 around which the outer shell 12 and inner rotation assembly 14 are journaled, as will be hereinafter set forth, and plurality of legs 20 extending radically outward in circumferentially spaced relation from the lower end of the tubular member 18. The tubular member 18 is telescoped over a supporting stanchion 22 which may be in the form of a pipe, and the tubular member 18 is slidingly supported on the stanchion 22 by suitable wheels or rollers 24 to facilitate vertical movement of the member 18 on the stanchion 22, as will be hereinafter set forth. The stanchion 22 is preferably supported in a suitable foundation 25 to provide adequate strength for the amusement device.

A suitable jack 26, preferably a hydraulic jack, is anchored in the foundation 25 underneath the outer end portion with an extension 28 extending upwardly into connection with the respective leg 20. The jacks 26 are operated simultaneously to raise and lower the landing gear and supporting structure 10, as will be described. A suitable shaped housing 30 is preferably secured around each of the landing gear legs 20 to provide a streamlined appearance. It may be noted that each of the legs 20 is preferably constructed out of a structurally strong member, such as an I-beam, and is secured to the lower end portion of the tubular member 18 by suitable braces 32 and plates 34 to assure a rigid and adequate connection of the legs 20 to the tubular member 18.

A pair of rollers 36 (see also Fig 3) are rotatably supported adjacent the other end portion of each leg 20 of the landing gear and are arranged to engage a circular track 38 (Fig. 2 and 4) for partially supporting the outer shell 20 and inner rotating assembly 14 as will be described. Also, a suitable drive motor 40 (Fig. 3) is mounted on one of the legs 20 of the landing gear and is connected through a suitable gear box 42 to one of the rollers 36 to rotate the outer shell 12 with respect to the landing gear and supporting structure 10. The roller 36 connected to the drive motor 40 may be suitably chained (not shown) to its companion roller 36 to assure an adequate drive connection between the drive motor 40 and the circular track 38.

The shell 12 (Fig. 2) is tubular in configuration, with the diameter of the central portion thereof substantially larger than the diameter at the opposite ends thereof, and is supported in an upright position to give the general appearance of two saucers placed face-to-face. The outer edge portion 44 of the shell 12 is preferably formed of partially transparent material, such as Plexiglas, and is illuminated from within (not shown) to provide a band of light around the central portion of the shell 12. The remainder of the shell 12 is formed of any desire opaque and relative strong material, such as aluminum-laminated Masonite sheets.

The shell 12 is supported on a frame generally designated by reference character 46 and illustrated in Figs. 2 and 4. The frame 46 is circular in plan, as viewed in Fig. 4, and is substantially U-shaped in cross-section (as shown in Fig. 2) to provide an upper horizontally extending portion 48 and a lower horizontally extending portions 50 which extend from adjacent the support-member 18 outwardly to the central portion of the shell 12. The frame 46 may be easily formed with industrial square steel tubing 52 formed into a truss with bracing of steel rods 54. With this construction, the frame 46 may be easily fabricated in sections for convenient assembly, or the entire frame 46 may be lifted off of the supporting member 18 and transported to another location.

Support of the frame 46 and the outer shell 12 is provided by the track 38 (previously mentioned) which is secured on the lower face of the lower horizontally extending portion 50 of the frame 46 in a position to engage the rollers 36 carried by the landing gear legs 20. Additional support for the frame 46 is provided by rollers 56 (Fig. 6) secured around the inner edge of the lower portion 50 of the frame, and rollers 58 secured around the inner periphery of both portions 48 and 50 of the frame. The rollers 56 are arranged in circumferentially spaced relation around the inner periphery of the frame 46 and engage in circular track 60 supported by the legs 20 of the landing gear. The track 60 may be an extension of the upper plate 34 shown in Fig. 3. The rollers 58 engage tracks 62 extending circumferentially around the supporting member 18 to accommodate any radial forces imposed on the frame 46. It will be understood that any desired number of the rollers 58 may be provided around the inner periphery of the frame 46 to provide the necessary support. It will thus be apparent that where the drive motor 40 is placed in operation, the rollers or wheels 36 operated by the motor 40 will engage the track 38 to rotate the shell 12 in on direction around the longitudinal axis of the supporting member 18. The rollers 56 will engage the track 60, and the rollers 58 will engage the tracks 62 during such rotation of the outer shell 12 and frame 46.

The inner rotating assembly 14 is generally annular-shaped as illustrated in Fig. 5, for movement around the supporting member 18 between the upper and lower horizontally extending portions 48 and 50 of the frame 46. The assembly 14 is also preferably constructed as a frame out of square steel tubing 52 formed into a truss with steel rods 54 for bracing, and is provided with a double conically-shaped framework 64 adjacent the supporting member 18. The framework 64 is provided to support a covering material 66 of any suitable type, such as the power unit for the craft. The covering material 66 may be corrugated if desired. The framework 64, as illustrated in Fig. 6 is also provided to support the rotating assembly 14 on the supporting member 18 and the frame 46. A plurality of rollers 68 are provided around the lower face of the framework 64, and a plurality of rollers 70 are provided around the upper face of the framework 64 to engage circular tracks 72 and 74 respectively, which are mounted on the frame 46. The rollers in each set of rollers 68 and 70 are provided in circumferentially spaced relation around the inner periphery of the rotating assembly 14. Additional rollers 76 and 78 are provided around the inner periphery of the framework 64 to engage tracks 80 extending circumferentially around the supporting member 18 to accommodate radial thrusts imposed on the central rotating assembly 14. It will be apparent that any desired number of rollers 76 and 78 may be provided around the inner periphery of the framework 64 to adequately support the rotating assembly 14.

I also prefer to support a plurality of conically-shaped members 82 in the outer edge portion of the central rotating assembly 14. Each conically-shaped member 82 may be easily formed out of a suitable sheet material such as laminated aluminum or plastic, and is supported at its opposite ends by suitable traunnions 84 to extend through the truss comprising the frame of the central rotating assembly 14. The conically-shaped members 82 are preferably provided in circumferentially spaced relation around the assembly 14, as illustrated in Fig. 5, and are positioned to move through simulated electro-magnets 86 supported around the frame 46, as illustrated in Fig 2 and 4. Each simulated electro-magnet 86 may be formed in horse shoe shape out of any suitable sheet material, and is provided with tubing or the like 88 around a portion thereof to simulated the winding of an electro-magnet. I further prefer to secure a plurality of plates 90 in spaced relation around the upper face of the rotating assembly 14 to simulated capacitor plates in a space craft. The plates 90 may be formed out of any suitable material, such as aluminum laminated Masonite, to provide a striking appearance.

The inner rotating assembly 14 is driven by a friction or dead wheel 92 pivotally supported on the tubular member 18, as illustrated in Fig. 6, engaging circular plate 94 and 96 carried by the inner rotating assembly 14 and the frame 46, respectively. The plates 94 and 96 are arranged in vertically spaced relation with sufficient distance there between to frictionally engaged opposite portions of the wheel 92. It will therefore be apparent that when the frame 46 is turned in one direction, the plate 96 will engage the periphery of the wheel 92 to drive the wheel 92 and in turn drive the central rotating assembly 14 in an opposite direction by frictional engagement of the wheel 92 with the plate 94. Therefore, the various conically-shaped member 82 will be moved successively through the simulated electro-magnetics 86 and give the appearance of the generation of electrical energy.

The cabin 16 is supported on the upper end of the tubular supporting member 18 and is rigidly secured to the member 18 by bracing 100 to move with the supporting member 18 and to be prevented from rotating with the shell 12 or rotating assembly 14. Additional support is provided by a plurality of rollers 101 carried by the frame 46 engaging a complementary track on the bottom of the cabin. The cabin 16 is constructed out of a suitable framework 102 covered by suitable sheet material 104, such as aluminum laminated with Masonite, on the outer surface of the framework and any other suitable material 106, such as Masonite, around the inner surface of the framework. It will be understood that substantially strong members 108 must be provided in the floor of the cabin 16 to adequately support passengers in the cabin. As illustrated in Fig. 7, a plurality of transparent windows 110 are provided adjacent the outer and inner peripheries of the floor of the cabin 16, through which passengers in the cabin may adequately view the inner rotating assembly 14 and the frame 46.

Passengers may either stand or sit in the cabin 16 and may gain entrance and exit from the cabin through suitable doors 112 as illustrated in Fig. 2. It will also be noted that the upper edge portion 114 of the outer shell 12 is extended upwardly to overlap the lower end portion of the cabin

16. A portion of the upper edge 114 of the shell 12 is removed, as at 116 in Fig. 1, such that passengers may enter the cabin 16 through the doors 112. Simulated port holes 118 are provided around the upper edge portion of the cabin 16 to further simulate an interplanetary space craft. It will be noted, however, that the port holes 118 are preferably covered with an opaque material on the inside of the cabin 16 to prevent the passengers from seeing familiar objects outside of the cabin 16.

The dome 120 is preferably provided in the top central portion of the cabin 16 and the under surface thereof is covered with a suitable material 122, such as cloth or the like, which will display a movie scene. A projector 124 is suitably mounted in the central portion of the floor of the cabin 16 to project an animated movie onto the screen 122 during operation of the amusement device. The movie displayed by the projector 124 is preferably an animated movie of heavenly bodies displayed on the screen 122 will appear to come closer to and move away from the passengers during operation of the amusement device to give the impression of interplanetary flight.

In summarizing the operation of the preferred amusement device, the passengers are directed into the cabin 16 through the opening 116 in the upper edge portion of the shell 12 and through the doors 112. The doors 112 are then securely fastened in closed position and the passengers are thereafter prevented from viewing any object outside of the amusement device during the simulated flight. The driver motor 40 is then placed in operation to rotate the shell 12 and frame 46 in one direction, which the friction wheel 92 drives the inner rotating assembly 14 in and opposite direction. Passengers in the cabin 16 will then view the movement of the inner rotating assembly 14 and the frame 46 through the windows 110 to receive the impression of watching the inner workings of a space craft. Also, suitable lighting effects (not shown) are preferably provided in the shell 12 to illuminated the moving parts. Simultaneously with rotation of the shell 12 and the inner rotating assembly 14, the jacks 26 are actuated to raise the supporting member 18 will be rather minor, but will be sufficient to give the sensation of rising to the passengers in the closed cabin 16. It will be observed that when the supporting member 18 is raised, the shell 12 and inner rotating assembly 14 are simultaneously raised to retain the vertical relationship between the cabin 16 and the remainder of the apparatus viewed by passengers in the cabin. Also, simultaneously with rotation of the shell 12 and rotating assembly 14, the movie is displayed by the projector 124 on the screen 122 on the dome of the cabin to give the passengers the impression of approaching one or more heavenly bodies. The jacks 26 are then operated in the opposite direction to lower the cabin 16 and the movie projector by the projector 124 may then provide an impression on the screen 122 that the passengers are returning to Earth.

From the foregoing it will be apparent that the present invention provides and amusement device which will give the impression and sensation to patrons or passengers of the device that they are taking an interplanetary flight. The device includes counter-rotating sections simulating the inner workings of a space craft and those moving sections may be easily viewed by passengers in the device. Also, the passengers are slightly raised during operation of the device to simulate flight from the Earth and a movie is simultaneously displayed to give the impression of approaching a heavenly body. It will also be apparent that the construction of the amusement device is such that the device may be easily disassembled and moved from one location to another. It will further be apparent that the present amusement device is simple in construction, may be economically manufactured and will have a long service life.

Changes may be made in the combination and arrangement of parts or elements as heretofore set forth in the specifications and shown in the drawings, it being understood that changes may be made in the embodiment disclosed without departing from the spirit and scope of the invention as defined in the following claims.

I claim:

1. In an amusement device simulating a space ride, the combination of: an outer tubular shell, the diameter of the central portion of said outer shell being substantially larger than the diameter at the opposite ends thereof, means for supporting the outer shell in an upright position with the largest diameter thereof extending horizontally, means for rotating the outer shell about its longitudinal axis, a plurality of simulated electro-magnets carried in circumferentially spaced relation in the outer shell, an annular-shaped frame rotatably supported concentrically in the outer shell, means for simultaneously turning said frame in a direction opposite to the rotation of the outer shell, conically-shaped members carried by said frame in positions for movement through the simulated electro-magnets in the outer shell, a passenger cabin having a floor therein, means for non-rotatably supporting the cabin above the outer shell with the floor of the cabin positioned within the upper end portion of the outer shell, and transparent windows in the floor of the cabin for viewing movement of the outer shell and said frame from the interior of the cabin.

2. An amusement device as defined in claim 1 wherein said means for supporting said outer shell comprises a tubular support member extending downwardly from the cabin through the outer shell and said frame, a base portion on the lower end of said tubular support member simulating a landing gear, cooperating rollers and tracks supporting the

outer shell on the base portion, and means for raising and lowering said base portion during rotation of the outer shell and said frame.

3. In an amusement device simulating a space ride, the combination of: a vertically extending supporting member, a passenger cabin mounted on the upper end of the supporting member and having transparent windows in the floor thereof, an outer shell extending downwardly and outwardly from the lower end portion of the cabin and then inwardly and downwardly toward the supporting member, a first frame extending radially inward from the outer shell and having a generally U-shaped cross section with upper and lower horizontally extending portions, means rotatably supporting said first frame on the supporting member, a second frame rotatably supported on the supporting member for rotary movement horizontally between the upper and lower horizontally extending portions of the first frame, and means for rotating said first and second frames in opposite directions to simulate movement from the inner workings of a space craft as viewed from the cabin.

4. An amusement device as defined in claim 3 characterized further to include at least one jack connected to said supporting member for raising and lowering the cabin and first and second frames during rotary movement of said frame.

5. An amusement device as defined in claim 3 wherein said supporting member is a tube, and characterized further to include a fixed stanchion telescoped into the supporting member for holding the supporting member vertical, legs extending outwardly in circumferentially spaced relation from the supporting member below the lower horizontal portion of the first frame simulating a landing gear for the device, rollers carried by each leg, a circular track on the lower horizontal portion of the first frame, arranged to ride on said rollers during rotation of the first frame, and a jack connected to each leg of the landing gear for raising and lowering the supporting member on the stanchion during rotation of said frames.

6. An amusement device as defined in claim 5 wherein said means for rotatably supporting the first frame on the supporting member includes a track around the supporting member opposite each of the upper and lower horizontal portions of the first frame, and a plurality of rollers carried by each of the upper and lower horizontal portions of the first frame in circumferentially spaced relation in positions to engage the respective track.

7. An amusement device as defined in claim 5 wherein said means for rotatably supporting the second frame on the supporting member comprises a pair of vertically spaced tracks around the supporting member, two sets of circumferentially spaced rollers carried by the second frame in positions to engage said tracks on the supporting member,

circular tracks on the upper and lower horizontal portions of the first frame, and circumferentially spaced rollers on the upper and lower faces of the second frame for engaging the last-mentioned circular frame.

8. An amusement device as defined in claim 3 wherein said means for rotating said frames in opposite directions comprises concentric annular plates secured around the first and second frames in vertically spaced relation adjacent the supporting member, a friction wheel carried by the supporting member in a position to engage said plates and drive the second frame in one direction upon rotation of the first frame in an opposite direction, means for rotating the first frame.

9. An amusement device as defined in claim 3 characterized further to include a movie projector in the cabin arranged to project a movie of heavenly bodies on the interior of the cabin and provide passengers in the cabin with a sensation of interplanetary space flight.

If you enjoyed this book, please write
for our free catalog. Send your name and
mailing address to:

Global Communications
P.O. Box 753
New Brunswick, NJ   08903

Email: mrufo8@hotmail.com

www.conspiracyjournal.com

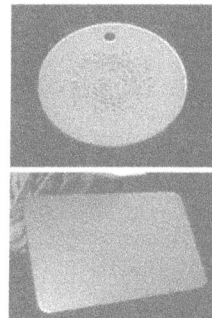